MW00678046

How To *Unleash The Promises of God* In Your Life

If the watchman sees the sword coming
and does not blow the trumpet to warn the people …
I will hold the watchman accountable …
Ezekiel 33:6

A Watchman.com Mission Statement

At A Watchman.com our mission is to illuminate God's Truth through the internet (Daily Readings & Online Classroom) and the publication of books, e-books, poetry, lyrics and games.

We believe that Jesus is the son of God who:

- Came and lived a perfect life on earth as our example.
- Died a brutal death to forgive us for our sins.
- He was raised by God to give an eternal hope and make us heirs to God's Kingdom.
- Loves us like no other.

This publication company was established to teach about this great love and help others become part of God's Kingdom.

God Has Promised Us Hope And He Has Delivered!

In the new book "Unleash the Promises of God", by an author known only as "A Watchman," God is sending readers a message of hope and encouragement. What impressed me most about this book is the feeling of direct contact with the Lord as I read the words. Each passage was an inspiring encouragement of how God is always watching and waiting on me. He is there for me and wants to be with me. It's all up to me whether or not I will seek him.

Reading about what God has planned for me and what it takes to unleash his promises, made it very difficult to sit still. As a can-do guy, when I get excited about something I want to learn as I go. As I read on, my desire to please God and unleash his promises got me up out of my seat and hitting the drawing board to figure out what I can do to best serve God. This book will be my guide and I am sure it will be yours too.

Capone DeLeon
Activist, Motivational Speaker, Entertainer Family Fiesta, Inc.

– Foreword –

Promises, promises. Everywhere we go someone is promising something they cannot deliver.

> "Lose 10 pounds while you sleep."
>
> "Cure your disease with herbal potions."
>
> "Follow these steps, and you will get rich overnight."
>
> "Buy this item and become popular."

This constant barrage of empty promises has led to the very frustrating pursuit of illusions. False hope and repeated disappointments have cultivated bitterness and cynicism. Years of chasing illusions have caused many to wonder what to believe. Despite this barrage of illusion, there is one whose words are true and everlasting. Our Heavenly Father has given us great and precious promises. He has promised us great blessings here on earth, a unique destiny to fulfill, hope for the future, and eternal life with Him.

He has so much he wishes to give us, yet we do not always receive His offer. Our enemy Satan is hard at work seeking ways to destroy us and keep us from receiving what God has promised. Many things we humans do "lock" us out from receiving all God desire to give us. This book was an assignment God placed on the heart of a watchman. It is a guidebook to help us all receive what God has planned. He wants us to receive all of His promises, but we must do so under His terms. We must fully examine our lives, and ask God to remove everything that goes against His will. We must put our full faith and trust in Him. We must give ourselves to His will and obey Him. We must develop an intimate, personal relationship with Him. As we take these steps, God will "unlock" His promises and give them freely.

My hope and prayer is that this book will help you unleash all that God has promised for your life. He has so much to give you. He stands waiting to give you all that He planned for your life. Are you ready to receive it?

James E. Thompson

– Introduction –

I am a Christian Watchman – a messenger of God. Through the power of the Holy Spirit, I believe in the death, burial, resurrection and ascension of our Lord and Savior Jesus Christ. Within these pages, my voice speaks God's truths.

I am also a spouse, parent, child, and a sibling of beloved brothers and sisters. I am a neighbor, a friend, a listener and a hearer. I am a business executive and a minister of the church. I use my voice to pray, my heart to love, and my hands to heal. I am like you. I have known pain and sorrow, joy and awakening. Just like you, I am on a journey of faith. Just like you, I have faltered, and the Lord has picked me up. I did not decide on my own to write this book. I was working, living and going along day by day when the Father placed in my heart the desire to compile these messages. As a servant of the most high God, I must obey His commands. My heart is heavy for all God's children who do not truly know Him and the power of His might … and because God is walking me through this path to victory and salvation, I want to share this journey with you.

I pray that these words, this Word of God, will change your life. The Holy Spirit knows your heart and He will instruct you according to where you are right now. He will reveal God's will for your life, and your heart and your mind will be opened.

I pray that each person who reads these messages is instructed, convicted and led by the power of the Holy Spirit. I thank God for His divine wisdom and anointing, for guiding me through the often arduous process of laying down these words, one by one, so that you may discover the spiritual purification that is yours through Christ Jesus.

– A Watchman

The secret of the kingdom of God has been given to you.
But to those on the outside everything is said in parables so that ...
they might turn and be forgiven! Mark 4:11,12

– CONTENTS –

CHAPTERS:

CHAPTER ONE

The Promises of God

> *Let us hold unswervingly to the hope we profess, for* ***He who promised is faithful****.*
> Hebrews 10:23

God promises peace, guidance, comfort, grace, joy, prosperity, love, mercy, healing, victory over the enemy, deliverance from sin, restoration, the Holy Spirit, answered prayer and much more. Are you experiencing the promises of God? If not, let's examine what could be the bottleneck that is stopping the flow of God's promises in your life.

God desires for His children to experience the Promised Land here on earth. I don't know about you, but I am tired of wandering aimlessly through the wilderness. Living life the same day by day … and nothing is changing or getting better. I am tired of collecting manna for just the daily eating, and on Fridays collecting a double portion in order to rest on the Sabbath day. You know what I mean … living from paycheck to paycheck ... robbing Peter to pay Paul ...one paycheck away from bankruptcy. I am ready to cross the Jordan and step on the flattened walls of Jericho to get all that God desires for me to have.

In Joshua Chapter 5, after crossing the Jordan River, the children of Israel thought they were ready to possess the Promised Land, but God instructed them of the process that they had to complete before they could enter in. God wanted them to purify themselves before entering the Promised Land. They were barred access to the land because of their unclean state. Their forefathers were disobedient to God, which caused their wilderness experience. There was a law or custom, which God had established for all Israelite male children – to be circumcised. But during their journey in the wilderness that law was disregarded by the Israelites. They had a generation of adult males who had not undergone the circumcision process and were not convicted by it until it was time to enter the Promised Land.

These men were grown before they went through purification. As for us, God is calling us to submit to the purification process before we enter the Promised Land. He is requiring a circumcision of our hearts. (Romans 4:28-29) God wants to clean the impurities out of our hearts – impurities such as strife, envy, bitterness, jealousy, hatred, pride and impure motives. The details of this process are discussed in the chapter, "Restoration."

God desires for us to serve Him with all our heart, soul, mind, body and spirit. He desires a closer relationship with you. God knows about the sin that is causing you to stumble and fall, especially the sin of pride. He has a word for all who are His concerning the spirit of pride which has waxed cold the hearts of men, rotted the religious community and sends an awful stench to the Father's nostrils. He desires that stench to change to a sweet aroma. In this book, you will understand God's will concerning His people returning to Him.

The promises of God are unleashed through prayer and fasting. He promises answered prayer and guidance to all issues of your life if you seek His face and His will for your life. God is the Promise Keeper. No one on this earth but God can keep all promises. He desires for you to die to self-will and be led by the Holy Spirit into His divine will.

Jesus came so we would have life more abundantly, not live like The Bundy's – "Married with Children." If you are not living the abundant life, you will know what is stopping you by the end of this book. God said He would restore everything the devil took from you and your family. Not only will He restore it, but also He promises to give you no less than double for your trouble. Wow! God is awesome! Let's get what God has desired for His people since the creation of the earth.

In this book, you will understand more about God's wisdom, guidance, love, generosity, provisions, pain, delights, disciplines and instructions for His people in this season. He is telling us, *Keep It Simple Saints*. He wants us to cut out the distractions that are causing confusion in our lives and hindering us from hearing His voice.

God desires for all His children to experience His promises. He wants us to understand that our faith, with His power, can do all things. God desires His children to come up higher in their spiritual walk with Him. He wants more of us and in return we get more of Him. Our primary reason for being obedient to God by pressing into His presence is because we love Him; we are obsessed with knowing more about Him; and we want to please Him.

Allow this book to delight you, minister to your soul and lead you into the perfect will of God. Submit to the Holy Spirit's process of changing you from Glory to Glory. Before God dealt with me, I was arrogant, selfish, self-centered and prideful. But after God pulled out the switch and tanned my legs, I realized how I really looked to Him and how He loved me enough to spend the time to alter my negative behavior. God loves those whom He chastens (an act of punishment intended to instruct and change behavior).

Beware of the giants in the land that will try to deter you from entering into the Promised Land. Much doubt and conflict will rise against you when trying to pursue God's will for your life, but do not fear the rejecters or the Promised Land haters – just press toward the prize. When they see how God will exalt you, they will be shamed. For God takes the foolish things of the world to shame the wise. (1 Corinthians 1:27) We must also stop allowing the world to dictate our destiny. When it comes to not receiving all God desires for us, we are our worse enemy. The children of Israel would not have been forced to wander the desert for 40 years if they had not been disobedient by lacking faith in God's sovereignty.

To experience all the promises God has for us, we must begin to take responsibility for our own actions. No more blame game, which started in the Garden of Eden. Adam blamed the woman God sent him; Eve blamed the serpent that seduced her. But God said, *You all must suffer the consequences for your actions.* The serpent was cursed to crawl on its belly forever. Eve was cursed to endure pain in child bearing and the enemy would always be hard after her (woman). Adam (man) was cursed to till the ground for his food by working for a living. They were all kicked out of the Garden. God is tired of us using our past or current relationships as excuses for our sins. We are all held accountable for our actions. Do not allow yourself or anyone else to hinder you from entering the Promised Land.

<u>The Promised Land of God includes Love.</u> If you have bitterness, hatred, strife or unforgiveness in your heart, you are not in the Promised Land.

<u>The Promised Land of God includes Forgiveness.</u> Are you still feeling guilty about a sin that was committed in your life by you or someone else? If so, you are not in the Promised Land.

<u>The Promised Land of God includes Salvation and Everlasting Life.</u> Are you sure of where you will spend eternity? If you are not sure of your salvation, you have not entered the Promised Land.

<u>The Promised Land of God contains the Holy Spirit and His presence.</u> Do you feel the presence of God in your life and does God's Spirit lead you in all that you do? If you have never felt God's presence or if you do not feel the Holy Spirit leading you, you are most definitely not in the Promised Land. The Promised Land is filled with God's Spirit. When His Spirit is not

leading you, you quickly know the difference. Then you must examine yourself by considering your ways, repenting and getting back in God's will. This is illustrated in Joshua Chapter 7 when Achan sinned (greed) and caused God to curse the Israelites and threaten to remove himself from them if they did not remove the issue that caused the curse. (Joshua 7:12)

The Promised Land of God has Peace. If you are worried, stressed, frustrated, afraid, perplexed, frazzled, then the Promised Land is not your current hometown. No need to fear, fret or worry because God has plenty of peace for everyone in the Promised Land. There you know without a shadow of doubt that God has everything under control and He will work all things out for your good. (Romans 8:28)

The Promised Land of God is saturated with Joy. Are you depressed, sad, angry or grumpy most of your waking hours? If so, you made a detour on your way to the Promised Land. God did not desire for us to be consistently sad or unhappy. The joy of the Lord is our strength. We must realize that our circumstances or issues of life do not dictate our joy – joy is God's gift to us. In the Promised Land there is no yielding to depression or allowing a constant case of the grumpies.

The Promised Land of God is Freedom. Are you enslaved to religious tradition, the sin of nature or the carnal man? Are you still battling with the addictions of alcoholism, lust, overeating, sugar, smoking, drugs, etc.? If so, God wants you to know that you are delivered in Christ Jesus, and the Promised Land is waiting for you. Believe and receive your deliverance.

The Promised Land of God has Growth. If you are stagnated in your walk with God, in your financial situation, in your relationships or in your church, you are not experiencing the fullness of God's provision. God designed us as a people to grow from Glory to Glory.

The Promised Land of God includes the Blessing. If you have not received the blessing of God, which is His anointing to fully execute His principles for your life, you have not reached your destination.

The Promised Land includes Prosperity. For God said, *Everything you do will prosper.* (Psalm 1: 3b) If you are not experiencing prosperity in every area of your life, you are not in the Promised Land. Prosperity is not just for finances – it also includes peace, joy and all the fruit of the Spirit. It is happiness in your home, on your job and at your church. Yes, God desires for us to have a prosperous life.

The Promised Land of God also includes Healing. God wants you to be made whole in every area of your life, including your health.

The Promised Land also offers answers to prayer. Have you prayed and prayed, but cannot hear from God? God delights in our communing with Him and His responding to us. Sometimes there are blockages in your communication with God. If that is so, you are not experiencing God's promise of answered prayers.

The Promised Land of God includes the foreknowledge that Christ will return and you are always standing ready for His coming. God promised Christ is going to return. If you have not yet settled in your heart that Christ can come at anytime, even during your lifetime, this book is especially for you.

If the Promised Land of God sounds too good to be true, you are partly right. It is too good, but it is also very true. God has endowed us with His power to live the Promised Land experience here on earth. This life is the dress rehearsal, which is preparing us for the new heaven and the new earth when Christ will return and reign over all.

There are rich blessings stored up for all who obey Him. God desires a relationship with His children. He wants us to operate under His will, not our own or someone else's. God is Love, Joy, Peace, Health, Forgiveness, Salvation, Freedom, Growth, Encouragement, the Blessing, Hearer, Responder and a Promise Keeper. He wants His children to experience these inherited traits and much more. Are you really experiencing all God has desired to give you? If not, read this book and have a highlighter handy. You will enjoy knowing that God had you in mind when He instructed me to write this book. This book will settle in the hands and hearts of people who are serious about getting closer to God and living in the fullness of God's Promises.

Life has many destinations, but there is only one path that leads to the Promised Land. You have to come out of Egypt. Give up the worldly lifestyle by surrendering your life to God. Then you must cross the Red Sea. No more trying to hold on to the worldly life and the cross. The Red Sea needs to close up for you, burying all of your past troubles and hurts. Then you must exit the wilderness – which requires giving up your "just existing" and stagnant lifestyle. Then you must cross the Jordan – which requires a cultivation of your faith. You must also be circumcised. This is the cleaning up of your heart by the Holy Spirit. Next you must march around the Walls of Jericho – which is an endurance builder and pride breaker. Can you run the race of a life lived for God and not get weary in well doing, or care what others think about you? Then you must give a large shout to allow God to collapse the obstacles in your life. Prayer is essential when trying to possess the land. You must ask, seek and keep knocking until your Promised Land experience with God is manifested.

As a Watchman, God has given me a word for this generation. **Bible** references, which correspond to the chapters, are located in Appendix A. If you are a person who must dissect this book for validity, please do so and God will reveal all truths. If it is not of God, it will not last, but if it is of God it will endure. I pray that all the readers of this book experience a true understanding, become committed to God and enter His Promised Land for their lives. Get ready to experience God's anointing and the release of His Promises in your life.

> *This day I call heaven and earth as witnesses against you that I have set before you life and death, blessings and curses. Now choose life, so that you and your children may live and that you may love the Lord your God, listen to His voice, and hold fast to Him. For the LORD is your life, and* ***He will give you many years in the land He swore to give to your fathers, Abraham, Isaac and Jacob.***
> (Deuteronomy 30:19-20)

Chapter Two

The Terminator

This chapter reveals the truth about Satan and his deception. Know the truth and the truth shall set you free!!! (Luke 10:17-19)

God knew you before you were formed. He knew who you would become and how you would be used to advance the Kingdom. The enemy was also in the huddle when the plays were designed. He took it upon himself to be the quarterback, but God said, *NO, I am the quarterback, playmaker and play caller up here.* Lucifer was full of pride; therefore, he was unhappy with God's decision to not let him control the offense. God put Lucifer out of the game and cast him out of heaven. But, there is a twist to the story. Lucifer, now known as Satan (the enemy, the devil) took the play book with him and started a defensive team to go up against the offense of God's plan for us. The terminator knows the plays and what position you play on God's team and he has come back through time to try and destroy you before you reach your destiny in Christ. (The fall of Satan: Luke 10:18; Isaiah 14:12-15).

The movie, "The Terminator," which starred Arnold Schwarzenegger, was a great illustration of how the enemy will do any and every thing to destroy the deliverer of a people. The terminator was thrust back to the past to abort the destiny of the man who would lead an army against the future robots. If you took note of the story line, the terminator did not come back to kill the man after he was born; he tried to kill his mother so that she would never give birth to the deliverer of his people.

Many of us had bad childhoods and our parents had an even tougher time. This generation is here for a very specific purpose. God has an appointed plan and assignment for our lives. He is ready for us to understand our true purpose for being here, and He wants us not to shy away from our destiny. God is going to judge us according to what we did and DID NOT do while here on earth. He will want to know why you did not carry out the assignment that you were tasked to do. Do you want to hear, *Well done, good and faithful servant...* (Matt 25:23) or *Depart from me, you who are cursed...*(Matt 25:41)? To do a job well you must first know its requirements. Then you must be trained for the job and execute the job with excellence and perseverance. God knows your job title, its requirements and how to train you to execute it. (Romans 8:29-30)

Don't allow the terminator's disruptive plans, past or present, to hinder your future. Use your past situations to build a positive ministry. If you were a drug addict, start a home to help rehabilitate drug addicts. If you were an alcoholic, start a ministry to assist recovering alcoholics. If you have experienced the deaths of loved ones, start a ministry to assist people with grief. If you had problem with lust and became pregnant as a teen, teach abstinence to youth. If you were sick or near death, teach of miracles, healing power and faith in God. If you were full of pride, selfishness, envy, strife and jealousy, write a book about purification, holiness and the refiner's fire. What the devil meant for evil, God is going to use for good!

Let's take a stroll through the **Word** and revisit some situations where the terminator was in action. Moses was set apart before he was born to deliver the Israelites from the hands of the Egyptians. Even before Moses was born, a plan by the terminator was in the works to kill all Israelite baby boys. The plan was then deposited in the heart of Pharaoh. What we must understand about the terminator is that he needs a host to complete his assignment. Don't allow yourself to be manipulated by the terminator to carry out his deceptive mission. Pharaoh had no idea that this thing was much larger than him. You know the end of the story ... Moses led the children out of Israel and completed the assignment which he was birthed to do. Yes ... the terminator was defeated.

Jesus was born to a virgin named Mary, but there was a plan in the works to destroy Him before He was born. The terminator showed up on the scene again and planted deception into the heart of King Herod to destroy the baby once the wise men found Him. But we all know how this story ended. The wise men were visited in a dream with a message from God, which revealed the deceptive plan of King Herod. Once again, the terminator lost the battle.

Oh yeah, let's not forget Joseph. His father favored Joseph, and his brothers were jealous. Joseph's own mouth caused the terminator to spring into action. If God has placed in your spirit His divine destiny for your life, do not go around bragging about it, because that is an open door for the enemy to step in and try to disrupt the plan. Joseph was thrown into a pit, picked up, dusted off and sold into slavery (similar to what our religious community has done with God's children, but we will get into that later in this book). Again, the terminator's plot was spoiled, because after Joseph got to Egypt, he later became second in command to Pharaoh.

Let's talk about Saul – later to be known as Paul. Saul was born into a religious, legalistic, and traditional environment. He was a Pharisee. He knew the letter of the law and taught it. Once Jesus came on the scene, he began to persecute and kill Christians for their belief in Jesus, the Christ. The terminator was on the scene early in Saul's life and used him as a host to execute his plan. Oh … but when Saul was met on the road by the Lord, he was transformed. Instead of Saul executing the terminator's plan, Paul executed Jesus' plan. The terminator met Paul again when he was persecuted and almost killed. He encountered the terminator when he was thrown in prison and sailed the high seas to clear his name. Paul and the crew were shipwrecked on an island and the terminator used a snake as a host (reminiscent of the garden) to poison Paul. Paul was imprisoned many times by the terminator, who tried to abort his mission. The terminator stalked Paul, who said, "For when I will do good, evil is ever present." You ask yourself why the terminator was hot on Paul's trail? Paul was sent to this earth by God to write the majority of the New Testament – the Word of God, which guides our lives today. Paul completed his mission and once again the terminator's plan was spoiled.

What about you? God has handcrafted you for a particular purpose on this earth and He desires for you to complete your assignment, but the terminator is always near. The terminator might have started with you as child. A parent or both parents may have abandoned you. He might have made you live a life of poverty to oppress and break your spirit. He may have caused childhood trauma in your life such as sexual, physical or mental abuse. He may have taken someone or something dear to you away to decay your support structure. He may still be lurking in your adult life by consistently condemning you of your past and sending you into depression and anxiety. He may get to you with the voice of insecurity and lack. He may have immersed you in yourself with selfishness, pride, envy and an, "I want to be happy" attitude. I am here to tell you that it is up to you to spoil the terminator's plan for your life.
You must first believe that God has a higher calling for your life than where you now find yourself. Also, you must seek God for your destiny. If there is anything or anybody who is causing you to stray from God, let them go! You never know whom the terminator is using for a host to abort your destiny in Christ.

Just when you think your backsliding days are over, the terminator says, "I'll be back!" The enemy is very crafty, patient and cunning. He has stalked you and knows your stronghold. For some of us it is smoking, alcohol, drugs, sex, overspending, overeating – then feeling tired and depressed, suffering fits of rage and anger (outbursts or internal quiet rage), speaking filthy language, being full of pride or manipulation, thinking or speaking negatively about others and lashing out at loved ones. The enemy will tap into your stronghold during the weakest times of your life. Always be alert in the spirit of your surroundings, and God will make sure the enemy does not ambush you. We are like pieces in a game. The enemy knows he loses the battle in the end, but during the first to third quarters he wreaks havoc – causing you to lose your focus, rendering you helpless and hopeless, seeming to abort your destiny. Do not get overwhelmed by the first three quarters, because what we do in the fourth quarter will determine how and where we spend our eternal life. Do not give up; do not forfeit your eternal peace.

When you get to the place where you know that God has heavenly angels going before you, covering you 24 hours a day and flanking you on the right, left, front, behind, above and beneath, then the terminator is running from you. Through the remaining chapters we will walk you out of Egypt across the Red Sea, through the wilderness and into the Promised Land / Kingdom living which God ordained for His people since the beginning of the earth. Just how fast you get to the Promised Land will depend on you. God said, *Everything is done and we have victory over the terminator*. But we must do some things to release the manifestation of what God has already completed.

Don't let the terminator steal your rightful place in God's Kingdom. Don't allow him to steal your joy, peace, money, love for others or happiness. Do not allow him to abort your destiny. He had me on the run for a while, but I stopped and looked my issues straight in the eye and said, "You will not pass here! Enough is enough!" I drew a line in the sand and told the terminator that he has no place in my family, my home, my friends, my church, my community, God's children or me!

Now I understand why the terminator was after my family and me so hard – and you will understand as you read this book. Now I know what God's divine destiny is for my life. Once you understand who you are in Christ Jesus, then no devil in hell can rob you of your destiny. You will press, fast, fight and pray to stay on track with God's will for your life.

You must understand the craftiness of the terminator. He will use any means necessary to rob, steal, kill and destroy your destiny. He does not care about your material goods or your money, but he is aware that this is an area of weakness for many people. If you speak to all that you own and say, "Stuff, I don't own you and you do not own me!" a feeling of release will come over you. That statement is telling God through your words and your heart that you surrender all, because all of it, all of *you*, belongs to God. Words spoken from the heart are life changing, because power is in the tongue.

The terminator also targets the gates to your physical body. God says to guard your eye gate, ear gate, mouth gate and reproductive gates. If we are truly pressing into God's divine will for our lives, we must cut off all entries for the terminator to slip in and try to disrupt the plan. *Resist the devil, and he will flee from you.* (James 4:7b)

The eye gate is the lighthouse to our body; it guides the body where to go and what to do once it gets there. We must release ourselves from pornography, books, magazines, movies and television shows that depict nudity, vulgarity, violence and other lifestyles outside of God's plan. The eyes send thought patterns to the brain. *What a man thinketh, so shall he be.* (Proverbs 23:7, KJV) The terminator knows that whoever controls the mind controls the body. We need to understand how to protect our thoughts from the terminator.

The terminator also uses the ear gate to deposit negative words and vile language into us. The music you listen to and the music videos you watch are all part of the terminator's plan to control your thoughts and abort your mission in life. Usually, music has a longer-lasting effect than just the three minutes it plays. Example ... driving to work, you hear a song and it's the last thing you hear before you park and enter your work place. You're walking into work and that song is playing over and over in your mind, and you start singing the chorus (which is the only part you remember). *The tongue has the power of life and death….* (Proverbs 18:21) Now what if you were listening to some inspirational music that exalts God and uplifts your spirit – how different would your day be?

The mouth gate is a powerful tool for the terminator to release destructive words. He deceives us into thinking it is okay to speak negatively, gossip or slander others. Even if the story is true, if it is going to cause damage to others it should not be said or read. Stay away from people who dredge up dirt on others and constantly speak negative words. God states clearly in the book of Matthew that we will be judged for every idle word that is spoken out of our mouths. You are on trial every time you open your mouth, so be careful what you say. (Matthew 12:36-37; 15:11) If you are one of those people, ask God to forgive you and take away the negative talk and gossip from your lips.

> *If we confess our sins, He is faithful and just to forgive us our sins and cleanse us of all unrighteousness.*
> (I John 1:9)

The reproductive gate is used by the terminator to steal, kill and destroy – especially females. In Genesis, God said there would be enmity (strife) between the woman and Satan. (Genesis 3:15) But ladies and gentlemen, we can stop the terminator dead in his tracks if we learn to control this major issue that is running rampant in our society. The issue is SEX, which God created as an awesome experience between a husband and a wife. But somehow we have perverted it. Sex outside of your marriage is the most ingenious plot from the terminator, because it leaves you with extra baggage from others, depleted, violated, condemned, empty, lonely, unfulfilled, suffering unwanted pregnancies and abortions and sometimes feeling hopeless. It rips families apart. I am talking about when it is all over and the partners have moved on to other prey. This plan of the enemy leaves emotional scars on males and females that take years to heal. Sometimes, little boys and girls are sexually scarred. The terminator is not sensitive. He does not care how young he has to start in order to abort the destiny of a person who is going to be used for God's glory. The terminator takes no prisoners or hostages; he just wants to kill, steal and destroy. (John 10:10) Remember, he was in the huddle when the plays were called out, so he knew what you were going to be before you or your parents knew. That is why it is critical for parents to understand that from the day your child hits the cold air coming out of the womb, the terminator launches his attack.

> *The dragon stood in front of the woman who was about to give birth, so that he might devour her child the moment it was born.* (Revelation 12:4)

Parents, because this is not about you, but about what God wants to do through you and your offspring, don't allow your selfish sexual desires to put your children in the reach of a person being used by the terminator. These are things we do not talk about in church, but they are killing, stealing, aborting or delaying the God-ordained destiny of our children. Don't be surprised when your teenage daughter comes home and announces she is pregnant, if you allowed some pedophile to "shack up" with you for your own sexual pleasures. Don't get in a huff if your son is accused of date rape, if you assisted the terminator by condoning or exhibiting a "sex is okay as long as you are protected" lifestyle to your son. If your child comes home and announces that he is gay, trace back to see whom you allowed in his space as a child. These behaviors don't happen unless they have been taught or fostered in your child, whether by TV, videos, movies, music, video games, the Internet or a lifestyle to which he was exposed. Be careful whom you allow in your child's space. Don't be so eager to push them on someone else – that very someone might be a host for the terminator. Your child's Godly destiny is at stake.

A word of wisdom if you are still trying to justify your current sexual choice – common-law marriages are not God's plan. That's just another term for "shacking up." Sex between same sex partners, married or unmarried, is not God's plan. Masturbation is not God's plan. Adultery, sleeping with someone outside of your own marriage, is not God's plan. Phone sex is not in God's plan. Computer online sex is not in God's plan. Sex between boyfriend and girlfriend is not in God's plan. Even looking at someone with lust in your heart is not God's plan.

> *You have heard that it was said, "Do not commit adultery." But I tell you that anyone who looks at a woman lustfully has already committed adultery with her in his heart.* Matthew 5:27-28

Fondling, kissing, getting heated up even if no intercourse occurs is not God's plan. **God said flee from temptation, not run to it!** We should all know that incest, child pornography and child molestation are not God's plan.

This is hard to read. It is hard for me to write, but yes, it is happening and God says, *Enough is enough!* Parents press and pray for God to protect and guide your children. We must pray that God helps us to control our sexual desires when they are not within His guidelines. Submitting to our sinful sexual feelings causes hurt – not sexual healing. Don't let the terminator use you to destroy or delay someone else's destiny.

We must keep our gates filled with the Spirit of God, or the enemy will come in and set up shop in our minds and hearts. (Ephesians 5:18-20) The terminator is like a computer virus. Once he has entered one of the gates, he spreads through the body and corrupts the entire system. Sometimes you get those unsolicited, dirty e-mails that try to seduce with words like, "Know the naked truth about Suzie," or "Honey Bunny wants to show you something." As soon as you click open the attachment, the virus penetrates your computer system, rendering it helpless to any instructions from the mouse or the keyboard. Do not allow your gates to be infiltrated by the terminator like a virus, rendering you deaf to God's voice or mute to His ear. Just don't click!

Above all else, guard your heart, for it is the wellspring of life. (Proverbs 4:23) The terminator will use our own issues and emotions to abort our destiny. How do you feel during your day? Angry? Frustrated? Depressed? These negative feelings are not of God. (Galatians 5:19-21) These are evil spirits the terminator has sent your way, because he can sense when you are reaching your boiling point. Never let the terminator see you sweat. He can smell fear, stress, frustration, and anger a mile away. He is standing guard – waiting for you to let your emotions explode so he can send in one of his demons to pounce and make you lash out at your spouse, children, friends, parents, boss, or even a motorist who cuts you off. Watch your emotions, because the terminator is always watching you. Sometimes it is hard to suppress these emotions. That is why we have the Holy Spirit to help us during these frustrating times. If you can't say a long prayer, just say, "Jesus, help me by removing these feelings I am experiencing right now." Don't let the terminator use you to destroy or delay your own destiny.

Once the terminator realizes he cannot get to you, he tries to divert your attention by attacking others in your family or your space. That is why intercessory prayer is vital in defeating the terminator and disrupting his plan. Once you get past a plot of the enemy, your discernment increases and you know when the terminator is using someone. Don't allow him to push your buttons. Press and pray for everyone in your space – even your enemies. List all the names and call them out to God in prayer. Pray that God's will for their lives will be manifested (see, feel, touch, smell and hear) now on earth, because it is already done in heaven! God wants us to know that His will for our lives was completed at the beginning of time, but we must pray for the manifestation – to feel, touch, smell, hear and see it.

God has already won the victory over the terminator. As sons and daughters of the most high God, we also have the victory, but we must know it – then take our rightful place in the Kingdom here on earth. We do not simply walk into a position for which we have not had proper training or experience. So it is with the Kingdom of God. He is preparing us for our royal positions as joint heirs with Christ, but first we must get past the roadblocks that the terminator has placed in our path. Tell the terminator, "Get thee behind me, Satan." *It is written: Do not put the Lord your God to the test.* (Matthew 4:10) God is living inside you and you are a joint heir with Christ, so yes, this Bible verse is for you. Put the terminator in his place. Do not allow the terminator to destroy the work that God has begun in you and your children. What if Mary, Joseph, Moses, Joshua, Abraham, David or Paul had given up? You know how the movie ended. The terminator was defeated and the child was born and completed his destiny. How does your story end?

Chapter Three

Christian in Drag

> *Examine yourselves to see whether you are in the faith; test yourselves. Do you not realize that Christ Jesus is in you–* ***unless, of course, you fail the test?***
> (2 Corinthians 13:5)

This chapter is not for the lighthearted or the holier than thou. This chapter is for the people who want the truth about salvation. I must illuminate the truth the way God has revealed it. A drag queen is a man who perpetrates by dressing like the opposite gender – but underneath he is still a man. God said that this is how many people are who sit in churches today. They think they are saved, but they are just "Christians in Drag." They dress up in religious clothing – quoting Bible verses, working themselves to death doing church work, and they may have the best hallelujah shout, but underneath they are still sinners and not justified by God.

God wants this message to be strong and hard because this is the key to whether you have eternal life or eternal death because you will experience one or the other. Is your name really in the Lamb's Book of Life?

> *But what does it say? "The word is near you; it is in your mouth and in your heart," that is, the word of faith we are proclaiming:* ***That if you confess with your mouth, "Jesus is Lord," and believe in your heart that God raised him from the dead, you will be saved. For it is with your heart that you believe and are justified, and it is with your mouth that you confess and are saved.*** (Romans 10:8-10)

Remember when you accepted Jesus into your heart? I am not talking about when Mama or Grandma forced you by giving you a gentle push toward the altar. Or when you were baptized – because baptism will not save you. Only through your confession of faith and believing in your heart are you saved. Example:

If a person accepted Jesus the Christ as Lord and Savior (meaning he confessed with his mouth and believed in his heart) on a third Sunday and abruptly died on Tuesday before baptism on the First Sunday, do you believe he would go to heaven or hell? Heaven, of course – because his name was immediately written in the Lamb's Book of Life when he confessed with his mouth and believed in his heart. ***For it is with your heart that you believe and are justified*** (Just as if you had never sinned). Yes, baptism is essential to the life of a believer, but it is not the key to eternal life with God.

True salvation comes with confession **AND** believing in your heart. We receive the Holy Spirit by believing in our hearts, for God knows the heart. **If you do not believe, you do not receive.** The Holy Spirit then leads us from Glory to Glory. Hence lies the problem: many are trying to change themselves without the aid of the Holy Spirit. They wonder why they are coming to church and still engaging in the same sinful acts. They want to change by becoming more like Christ, but they know something is missing. Some are not led by the Holy Spirit to change, because IT IS NOT IN THEM! We need to know without a shadow of a doubt that we are saved before Christ comes for His Church.

> *..."Brothers, you know that some time ago God made a choice among you that the Gentiles might hear from my lips the message of the gospel and believe.* ***God, who knows the heart, showed that he accepted them by giving the Holy Spirit to them,*** *just as he did to us.* (Acts 15:7-8)

> *And you also were included in Christ when you heard the word of truth, the gospel of your salvation.* ***Having believed, you were marked in him with a seal, the promised Holy Spirit,*** (Ephesians 1:13)

> *But the Counselor, the Holy Spirit, whom the Father will send in my name, will teach you all things and will remind you of everything I have said to you.* (John 14:26)

As the Titanic was sinking, there was a priest on board going about preaching the Gospel of Jesus Christ and leading many to Jesus. When those new believers died during that tragedy, I don't believe they went to hell. I believe God accepted them into heaven. So please understand that baptism does not save you! Also church membership and affiliation do not save you. Let's take a look at the Bible verses concerning baptism and being saved.

> *When the people heard this, they were* ***cut to the heart*** *and said to Peter and the other apostles, "Brothers, what shall we do?" Peter replied, "Repent and be baptized, every one of you, in the name of Jesus Christ for the forgiveness of your sins. And you will receive the gift of the Holy Spirit."* Acts 2:37-38

In Acts 2:37 the phrase "cut to the heart," reflects both belief in Jesus and regret over former rejection. This tells us that the people were convicted in their hearts to believe in Jesus Christ. In verse 38, Peter was following the message of John the Baptist, who came before Jesus, "Repent and be baptized." There must be sincere repentance before salvation takes place.

> *When the apostles in Jerusalem heard that Samaria had accepted the word of God, they sent Peter and John to them. When they arrived, they prayed for them that they might receive the Holy Spirit,* ***because the Holy Spirit had not yet come upon any of them; they had simply been baptized into the name of the Lord Jesus.*** Acts 8:14-16

Philip was in Samaria preaching the good news and many of the Samarians, including a sorcerer named Simon, accepted the gospel and were baptized. These people were infatuated with sorcery and magic; therefore they followed Simon until Philip came along with the true Power of God, the Holy Spirit. But don't you know – we can do right things, but when we do them with impure motives, they are not effective. Remember, God knows the heart. Many of these followers were baptized in water but the Holy Spirit had not clothed them. They were just "Christians in Drag." If you read on through to verse 18, you can see Simon's true motives. He wanted God's power, but he wanted to buy it.

> *Then Peter and John placed their hands on them, and they received the Holy Spirit. When Simon saw that the Spirit was given at the laying on of the apostles' hands, he offered them money and said, "Give me also this ability so that everyone on whom I lay my hands may receive the Holy Spirit." Peter answered: "May your money perish with you, because you thought you could buy the gift of God with money!* ***You have no part or share in this ministry, because your heart is not right before God.*** Acts 8:17-21

Simon's heart was not right before God; therefore he did not receive the Holy Spirit. Don't you know that many people join churches and become baptized for the wrong reasons? They want to brag about their church affiliation, or they want to be a deacon in the most popular church in the city because it looks good on their resume. They join because they are trying to get the attention or affection of a romantic interest. They want to get close to the most popular pastor in the city or country. They are not truly seeking God, but the things of God, which His children possess. Yes, the power of God draws people to the church, but if their motives are not pure, they never experience the Holy Spirit of God operating in their own lives; they are just pew warmers and "Christians in Drag."

> *While Peter was still speaking these words, the Holy Spirit came on all who heard the message. The circumcised believers who had come with Peter were astonished that the gift of the Holy Spirit had been poured out even on the Gentiles. For they heard them speaking in tongues and praising God.* ***Then Peter said, "Can anyone keep these people from being baptized with water? They have received the Holy Spirit just as we have."*** *So he ordered that they be baptized in the name of Jesus Christ. Then they asked Peter to stay with them for a few days.* Acts 10:44-48

Peter was preaching about Jesus Christ and *the Holy Spirit came on all who heard the message.*
In verse 47, Peter clearly states that these believers had received the Holy Spirit and had not been baptized. It was their hearts that allowed them to believe the gospel and receive the Holy Spirit even before they were baptized by water.

> *Paul said, "John's baptism was a baptism of repentance. He told the people to believe in the one coming after him, that is, in Jesus." On hearing this, they were baptized into the name of the Lord Jesus. When Paul placed his hands on them, the Holy Spirit came on them, and they spoke in tongues and prophesied.* Acts 19:4-6

These believers were baptized in John's Baptism, a baptism of repentance, and after believing on Jesus Christ, they received the Holy Spirit. John the Baptist clearly preached:

> *I baptize you with water for repentance. But after me will come one who is more powerful than I, whose sandals I am not fit to carry.* ***He will baptize you with***

the Holy Spirit and with fire. Matthew 3:11

One summer, when I was about nine years old, I remember visiting my grandparents and being baptized at their church. When I returned home, my parents joined a different denomination from my grandparents and the new church told my parents that I needed to be baptized again because my first baptism was not done in the right denomination. Religious factions and traditions have confused so many saints; they are not sure what to believe about true salvation.

True salvation came to me when I truly understood my profession of faith. I understood why I confessed with my mouth, "Jesus is Lord," and believed in my heart that God raised Him from the dead. This time, I was alone with God and gave my life to Him with conviction in my heart. Then I felt His presence. The Holy Spirit's presence is felt when true salvation takes place.

> *Brothers, you know that some time ago God made a choice among you that the Gentiles might hear from my lips the message of the gospel and believe. God, who* ***knows the heart****, showed that he accepted them by giving the Holy Spirit to them, just as he did to us.* Acts 15:7-8

> *And you also were included in Christ when you heard the word of truth, the gospel of your salvation.* ***Having believed, you were marked in him with a seal, the promised Holy Spirit.*** Ephesians 1:13

> *But the Counselor, the Holy Spirit, whom the Father will send in my name, will teach you all things and will remind you of everything I have said to you.* John 14:26

Do not confuse religious rituals and traditions with true salvation. There are many traditions that are not based on the Word of God. In order to receive true salvation, the Word of God tells us

> ***That if you confess with your mouth, "Jesus is Lord," and believe in your heart that God raised him from the dead, you will be saved. For it is with your heart that you believe and are justified, and it is with your mouth that you confess and are saved.*** Romans 10:9-10

Which came first, the chicken or the egg? Which comes first, the confession with the mouth or the belief in the heart? For some, it is the belief in their hearts that produces the convicted confession from the mouth. For others, it is the confession with the mouth that later produces the belief because the "power of life and death are in the tongue." You may not believe or understand it when you confess Jesus as Lord, but once you put that confession in the atmosphere with your mouth, the evidence of believing in your heart will eventually emerge. In some cases, it may be years later. Eventually you believed in your heart, and with that belief came the indwelling of the Holy Spirit. I was in the latter group.

We are born into sin, but through salvation we receive the Holy Spirit and He guides us to change and true repentance. Many who are in the church are not saved because they act contrary to the Holy Spirit and they cannot help it. They are "Christians in Drag" because they confessed with their mouths, but did understand or believe in their hearts. There is a conjunction in that Bible verse which states,.. a*nd believe in your heart.* God said because many did not believe, they did not receive the Holy Spirit and only by Him can a person change from Glory to Glory. God looks on the heart of man to see his sincerity. He is not as concerned with the outward person as He is concerned with your heart.

> ***The good man brings good things out of the good stored up in his heart, and the evil man brings evil things out of the evil stored up in his heart. For out of the overflow of his heart his mouth speaks.* (Luke 6:45)**

God knows that if your heart is purified, the outward man will follow.

Jesus warned us there would be weeds ("Christians in Drag") among us, but in the last days, God will reveal these weeds so that His wheat – the true believers – may flourish. "Christians in Drag," beware ... you might fool your pastor, Sunday school teacher, spouse, parents, church members, and even yourself, but you cannot fool God.

> *"An enemy did this," he replied. The servants asked him, "Do you want us to go and pull them up?" "No," he answered, "because while you are pulling the weeds, you may root up the wheat with them. Let both grow together until the harvest. At that time I will tell the harvesters: First* ***collect the weeds and tie them in bundles to be burned;*** *then gather the wheat and bring it into my barn."* (Matthew 13:28-30)

Jesus also warns us against the religious spirit, yeast, which inflates the issues of the church but does not have any substance. He says from such to turn away and do not fellowship with them. These people are modern day Pharisees and Sadducees, who are bound to work, and not to the grace of God. (Matthew 16:6) As God prepares His true believers by the purging, pruning, refiner's fire or circumcision of the heart, the truth will surface about these persons. We, as believers by the discernment of the Holy Spirit, will become more aware of their motives and their hearts. Do not be like the religious factions, having a form of godliness and denying the power of God by not yielding to His instructions for their lives. Hear God's voice and follow it even when it goes against a religious tradition you were taught as a child. When there are no more programs to produce, no more choir rehearsals, no more usher board meetings, no more committee meetings, no more deacon and trustee board meetings, no more minister meetings and no more church buildings standing, where will you be? The Spirit has informed me that someone will read this and "religiously" quote:

> *Upon this rock, I will build my church and the gates of hell shall not prevail against it.* (Matthew 16:18)

Yes, this Bible verse is true, but the church is not the buildings we serve in nor is it the things we do. The church is inside of us.

> *Do you not know that your body is a temple of the Holy Spirit, who is in you, whom you have received from God?* (1 Corinthians 6:19)

Now back to the question, where will you be when all of the church works are gone? If your answer is "disconnected," "lost" or "that will never happen," then take heed.

> *Not everyone who says to me, "Lord, Lord," will enter the kingdom of heaven,* ***but only he who does the will of my Father who is in heaven****. Many will say to me on that day, "Lord, Lord, did we not prophesy in your name, and in your name drive out demons and perform many miracles?" Then I will tell them plainly, "I never knew you. Away from me, you evildoers!"* (Matthew 7:21-23)

Do the will of the Father in heaven. Make sure you have a relationship with God and your faith is grounded in Him, not just the works of your church.

Let's take a look at some characteristic traits of a "Christian in Drag."

You <u>MIGHT</u> be a Christian in Drag if …

– You state in church meetings or any other meeting, "I am playing the devil's advocate." The devil does not need any advocates; he has enough helpers. You are either for God or against Him. There is no middle ground!

– You complain about every positive move your church or pastor is trying to accomplish. Confusion is not of God. The enemy comes to divide and conquer.

– You say, "God gave us a right mind to think and make our own decisions." This means you don't trust God to lead you to the correct decision. The Word says that His ways are higher than our ways, even as the heavens are from the earth. Therefore, we follow the Proverb which states, "Trust in the Lord with all your heart and lean not to your own understanding (right mind). In all ways acknowledge Him and He will direct your paths. I know why many of us do not follow this Bible verse and would prefer to use the above excuse about our own right mind, because we do not have an ongoing relationship with the Father; therefore we do not feel comfortable asking Him about everything. Also we are afraid of the answers He will give, which in some cases challenge our flesh.

– You constantly judge others, but find no fault in yourself. God warns us against judging others, for when we judge, we are trying to usurp God's position, because He is the only Judge. We all know what happened to Satan when he tried that stunt. God says, *Judge and you shall be judged.* (Matthew 7:1) However you judge others, that is how the Father will judge you.

– You do not have power over Satan. Is the enemy attacking and winning the battle in your life or are you beating Satan down? Christians have power over the enemy through Jesus the Christ.

> *"He who listens to you listens to me; he who rejects you rejects me; but he who rejects me rejects him who sent me." The seventy-two returned with joy and said, "Lord, even the demons submit to us in your name." He replied, "I saw Satan fall like lightning from heaven.* ***I have given you authority to trample on snakes and scorpions and to overcome all the power of the enemy; nothing will harm you.*** *However, do not rejoice that the spirits submit to you, but rejoice that your names are written in heaven."* Luke 10:16-20

– You have never experienced or felt the presence of the Holy Spirit. The Holy Spirit is not a silent partner in the Trinity, because His presence is felt when He is near. Everyone who has accepted Jesus Christ as Lord has Him living inside.
– You never experience joy or peace in your life. A constant worrisome spirit and negative attitude are not of God. He gives joy and peace that the world and the pressures of life cannot take away.
– You have tried to change your bad habits to become a better person and it is not working. God made it very clear that we cannot change our sinful nature. Only by the assistance of the Holy Spirit can those negative sinful behaviors be altered and sinful desires be stripped from our hearts. It is like dieting – as soon as you lose a few pounds, you begin to eat the same bad foods and gain all the weight back, sometimes more, because you are discouraged and depressed. Trying to change your sinful nature without the Holy Spirit is like dieting. Your bad habits change for a while, but as soon as the world throws you a curve, you are back at it again, but this time even worse because now you are discouraged, depressed and depleted.
– You cherish attending church meetings to get your point across

more than you cherish your prayer time with God.

- You only like to pray when others can hear your eloquent speech and never in private with God.
- You have something to complain about constantly and are never happy or content.
- You give so that others can see and reward you openly instead of relying on God to pat you on the back. God will reward you openly for the things you have done in secret. Stop bragging about what you have done for others.
- You think only about yourself and your family's well being. You have no desire to see others prosper greater than you. The Word says you cannot serve God and material things. Are you serving God by helping others or are you hoarding your prosperity for yourself?
- You do not tithe because you think the church or pastor is pilfering the money. The Word states that you are to give tithes and offerings, as God has prospered you. This principle alone is why many are still living from paycheck to paycheck. The tithe belongs to God. Pray and ask God where He would have you to sow your tithes.
- You hate attending church, but you go because someone forces you to attend every week. I rejoiced when they said to me, "Let us go into the House of the Lord."
- You are on patrol at church to see what everyone is wearing and doing in order to steal their joy by informing them of the dress code. Instead of allowing them to worship God and allow Him to gently guide them in their choice of attire.

There is hope in Christ Jesus through salvation. Do not let this day go by if you are uncertain of your salvation, because Jesus is coming for His people. DON'T GET LEFT BEHIND!

> *The Bridegroom is coming and the Bride is not adorned.* Matthew 25:10-13

What would you reply if you were asked, "If Christ came today, would you go to live eternity with God?" Make your response between 1 and 10, with 10 as the highest assurance and 1 as the least sure. What number would come to your mind concerning your salvation? Stop here and think about it.

If the number 10 was the first thing in your thoughts, then you are totally assured of your salvation, but if you thought of anything less than 10, you might be a "Christian in Drag." What is holding your heart and mind from a 10? Is it that you are not really saved, not sure, or you believe you are saved but there is some sin in your life keeping you from assuredly, positively and unequivocally saying, YES I AM GOING TO BE WITH GOD!!!!

Many believers who respond with anything less than a 10 are usually backsliding or living a lifestyle contrary to God's word. If this is you, please read the chapter on "Restoration," about restoring a right relationship with God. Please do not misinterpret the above statement. Your works will not get you to the Kingdom of God. You must be born again to enter into the Kingdom of God.

> *Jesus answered, "I tell you the truth, no one can enter the kingdom of God unless he is born of water and the Spirit. Flesh gives birth to flesh, but the Spirit gives birth to spirit. You should not be surprised at my saying, `You must be born again.' The wind blows wherever it pleases. You hear its sound, but you cannot tell where it comes from or where it is going. So it is with everyone born of the Spirit."* John 3:5-8

Here is a helpful Salvation equation:
Faith - Works = Death (faith without works is dead) James 2: 14-18
Works - Faith = Nothing (works without faith in Jesus Christ is worthless) Isaiah 64:6
Faith + Works = Salvation (confession and believing) Romans 10:9

The Holy Spirit comes to those who have received the Son of Man. Many claim to have received Him but in their hearts they have not. The Holy Spirit is moved by the belief in their hearts. The Holy Spirit can lead you to Jesus but cannot make you drink of the living water. The choice is yours. "You can lead a horse to water, but you can't make him drink." You must activate your faith by receiving Jesus as Lord and Savior.

Trade in your drag clothes for the anointing (the real thing). Be clothed in the Holy Spirit.

"The Perfect Gift"
I offer you a gift that will never get damaged, stolen or lost.
This gift will provide for, take care of, and love you for the rest of your life.
Also it does not cost you anything but it is worth so much.
I offer you the perfect gift of Jesus the Christ.
If you would like to receive this perfect gift, with a sincere heart repeat this prayer:

> Dear God,
> Please forgive me of my sins. I confess with my mouth and I believe in my heart that Jesus the Christ is Lord and that God has raised Him from the dead. In my heart, I accept the gift of God, which is life through Jesus the Christ. In Jesus' name, I pray.
> Amen

Congratulations! You now have the most perfect gift of all, Jesus the Christ. By believing that Jesus is Lord, you have nothing to lose, but oh so much to gain! Now share your gift with others. By: "A Watchman"

CHAPTER FOUR

Woe!

Now that you have traded in your drag clothes for the Holy Spirit, let's talk about how to press behind the veil into the presence of God. Let's get to the point – because the days of sugar coating the Word are over. God wants to warn us about a few "**quid pro woes.**"

> *For the sinful nature desires what is contrary to the Spirit, and the Spirit what is contrary to the sinful nature. They are in conflict with each other, so that you do not do what you want. But if you are led by the Spirit, you are not under law. The acts of the sinful nature are obvious: sexual immorality, impurity and debauchery; idolatry and witchcraft; hatred, discord, jealousy, fits of rage, selfish ambition, dissensions, factions and envy; drunkenness, orgies, and the like.* ***I warn you, as I did before, that those who live like this will not inherit the kingdom of God.*** Galatians 5:17-21

In the book of Galatians, Paul warns the church about the works of the flesh (their sinful nature) and how that affects their position in the kingdom of God. This warning applies to us today. Here are some things that will keep us from inheriting the Kingdom of God:

<u>Adultery</u> – The act of unfaithfulness in marriage that occurs when one of the marriage partners voluntarily engages in sexual intercourse with someone other than his or her spouse. And if you have lust in your heart for another, that is considered adultery in the eyes of God.

> *You have heard that it was said, "Do not commit adultery." But I tell you that anyone who looks at a woman lustfully has already committed adultery with her in his heart.* Matthew 5:27-28

My son, pay attention to my wisdom,
listen well to my words of insight,
that you may maintain discretion
and your lips may preserve knowledge.
For the lips of an adulteress drip honey,
and her speech is smoother than oil;
but in the end she is bitter as gall,
sharp as a double-edged sword.
Her feet go down to death;
her steps lead straight to the grave.
She gives no thought to the way of life;
her paths are crooked, but she knows it not.
Now then, my sons, listen to me;
do not turn aside from what I say.
Keep to a path far from her,
do not go near the door of her house.
Proverbs 5:1-8

Beware of the tempting spirit of adultery. Do not give room to the smooth talker, walker or giver; their evil ways will be revealed in time. You will be giving in to sin by allowing the evil one to control your body and your possessions. Your mind, body, spirit and soul will eventually come to itself, like the prodigal son, by mourning the very sin you committed. Just when you are on the verge of destruction, you will turn to God and repent of your infidelity. It is best not to indulge. Sin spreads through the mind, body, spirit and soul like a virus. Most of us attempt to keep our computers virus-free by running anti-virus software and not opening e-mail from unknown sources. But sometimes, **because of curiosity,** we "click" and the virus quickly takes hold of our CPU (Central Processing Unit), rendering it helpless to our commands. Now the system is at the mercy of the destructive virus. That is exactly how sin takes root in us. We must flee from temptation, not run to it. **Just don't click.** Your love, affections, effort and finances should be poured into your spouse and your household, not the enemy's camp. Love, cherish and respect your spouse. Stay with the mate whom God created and set-aside just for you. The pain of repentance is not worth the few seconds of sexual enjoyment.

> *At the end of your life you will groan,*
> *when your flesh and body are spent.*
> *You will say, "How I hated discipline!*
> *How my heart spurned correction!"* Proverbs 5:11-12

Fornication – Various acts of sexual immorality, especially being a harlot or whore. Engaging in sex outside of your marriage – husband & wife, male and female. No, common law marriage is not legal in God's sight. This is just another term for "shacking up." Homosexuality is not in God's plan.

> *Because of this, God gave them over to shameful lusts.* ***Even their women exchanged natural relations for unnatural ones. In the same way the men also abandoned natural relations with women and were inflamed with lust for one another. Men committed indecent acts with other men, and received in themselves the due penalty for their perversion.*** *Furthermore, since they did not think it worthwhile to retain the knowledge of God, he gave them over to a depraved mind, to do what ought not to be done. ... Although they know God's righteous decree that those* ***who do such things deserve death****, they not only continue to do these very things* ***but also approve of those who practice them****.* Romans 1: 26-28,32

> *Do not know that the wicked will not inherit the kingdom of God? Do not be deceived: Neither the sexually immoral nor idolaters nor adulterers nor male prostitutes nor* ***homosexual offenders*** *nor thieves nor the greedy nor drunkards nor slanderers nor swindlers will inherit the kingdom of God.* 1 Corinthians 6: 9-10

Uncleanness / Impurity – That which is defiled. This implies our internal state, such as unclean thoughts and the impure motives behind our actions.

Lewdness / Lasciviousness / Debauchery / Indecency / Sensuality – An unbridled expression of sexual urges. Sometimes refers to the especially heinous crime of brutal gang rape that results in murder. Most often lewdness is used figuratively for idolatry. Since the cults of many of Israel's neighboring peoples were fertility cults that employed sexual acts as part of worship, the application of lewdness to idolatry or unfaithfulness is easily understood. These are unbridled urges, which cause adults to rape little children, husbands to rape their wives, incest, date rape and other monstrous sexual crimes. These are not in God's plan.

Idolatry – Greed and covetousness, the deifying of self and other created things instead of God. In other words, putting anyone or anything before God in your life, including yourself. Selfishness is running rampant in our society and is a form of idolatry.

> *Put to death, therefore, whatever belongs to your earthly nature: sexual immorality, impurity, lust, evil desires and greed,* ***which is idolatry***. (Colossians 3:5)

Sorcery / Witchcraft – The power gained from the assistance or control of evil spirits, especially for divining. Attempting to contact supernatural powers to determine answers to questions hidden to humans and usually involving the future. Psychic hot lines or the practice of magic. If you are calling a psychic hot line, you are acting against God's plan. Practicing or reading about magic is against God's plan. No need to call Miss Cleo's Psychic hot line or allowing your children to read novels on witchcraft. God's Spirit will reveal to us the things we need to know.

*They sacrificed their sons and daughters in the fire. They practiced **divination and sorcery** and sold themselves to do evil in the eyes of the LORD, provoking him to anger. So the LORD was very angry with Israel and removed them from his presence.* (2 Kings 17: 17-18)

*He sacrificed his own son in the fire, practiced sorcery and divination, and **consulted mediums and spiritists**. He did much evil in the eyes of the LORD, provoking him to anger.* (2 Kings 21:6)

*"So I will come near to you for judgment. I will be quick to testify against **sorcerers**, adulterers and perjurers, against those who defraud laborers of their wages, who oppress the widows and the fatherless, and deprive aliens of justice, but do not fear me," says the LORD Almighty.* Malachi 3:5

Hatred / Enmity – A strong reaction, a feeling toward someone considered an enemy, as well as loving someone less than another. We should love everyone, even our enemies.

But I tell you who hear me: Love your enemies, do good to those who hate you, bless those who curse you, pray for those who mistreat you. Luke 6:27-28

God allows us to hate sin, but not the sinner. You must understand that only by the power of the Holy Spirit can we love someone who has harmed us.

Contention / Variance / Discord / Dispute / Strife – The fact or state of being in disagreement. A quarrelsome spirit. Someone who constantly has something negative to say and enjoys causing conflicts between others. You know the type – instigators. These people clasp onto gossip and spread it like wild fire. Stay clear of this type. I remember my grandmother used to say, "If you can't say something nice, don't say anything at all!"

Jealousies / Emulation / Envy – A painful or resentful awareness of another's advantage joined with the desire to possess the same advantage. It may involve wanting someone else's material or social status to the point of resenting them. Stop trying to keep up with the Jones' and pretending to be something you are not! Just because they bought a new HDTV does not mean you need to charge one and put yourself in deeper debt. One thing I have learned by working in the technology field for more than14 years is that technology changes every few months. The life cycle of flashy new products has shortened over the years, and faster than you can buy the latest and greatest, the newer model is already in production. Do not go into debt trying to keep up with technology. "You shall not covet."

Outburst of Wrath / Anger – Having fits of rage. Being ill or short tempered. My friends, we need to grow up and stop the adult temper tantrums. As my children have learned at school, "You get what you get and you don't throw a fit!" Once again, God has allowed us to hate sin and injustice, but He does not allow us to have fits of rage. We need to control our tempers. "Peace be still."

Selfish ambitions / Selfishness – Concerned excessively or exclusively with one's self: seeking or concentrating on one's own advantage, pleasure or well being, without regard for others. We have become lovers of ourselves.

> *But mark this: There will be terrible times in the last days.* ***People will be lovers of themselves****, lovers of money, boastful, proud, abusive, disobedient to their parents, ungrateful, unholy, without love, unforgiving, slanderous, without self-control, brutal, not lovers of the good, treacherous, rash, conceited, lovers of pleasure*

> *rather than lovers of God.* (2 Timothy 3:1-4)

We are always seeking the things that will make us happy even when it might hurt others in the process. "I want a new car, new golf clubs, new dress, new pair of shoes, new suit, new living room furniture or the latest surround-sound technology equipped with a plasma HDTV flat screen, even though it may strain our finances." "I want to be satisfied sexually with someone other than my spouse." "I'll swindle money from my customers to grow my bank account." "I can degrade, disgrace or discredit another person to make myself look good." "If they don't do it my way, then it's wrong." "How dare they not come or call when I say so." "No one appreciates me and the things I do." Does this sound like you? Stop allowing your selfish feelings to get in the way of God's plan for your life. Let God affirm you. Do not rely on others for affirmation, because people will let you down. We are human, but God is sovereign.

<u>Dissension / Sedition / Division</u> – Rebellion against lawful authority. Modern translations are more accurate in using "dissension." Relationships among believers rather than against a government are the apparent meaning. Causing division in churches, homes or at the work place.

<u>Heresies / Factions / Party Spirit</u> – This refers to groups which threaten the harmonious relations of the church. Also refers to false prophets or false teachings contrary to the true teaching about Christ.

<u>Murder</u> – To kill someone physically, mentally or spiritually. You can kill another's spirit and mental health by the things you say and/or do to them.

> *Anyone who hates his brother is a murderer, and you know that no murderer has eternal life in him.*
> 1 John 3: 15

Some of us are killing ourselves by our lifestyles and our eating habits. The doctor has warned us and some of us have heard from God, but we continue to commit suicide. Yes, this is deep but real. You cannot justify murder of self or others.

<u>Drunkenness</u> – A state of dizziness, headaches and vomiting resulting from drinking alcoholic beverages. A state of intoxication. Drunkenness is a pagan custom, not a Christian one. (1 Peter 4:3) Drunkards are among these who will not "inherit the kingdom of God."

> *Do not be deceived: Neither the sexually immoral nor idolaters nor adulterers nor male prostitutes nor homosexual offenders nor thieves nor the greedy nor **drunkards** nor slanderers nor swindlers will inherit the kingdom of God.* 1 Corinthians 6:9-10

<u>Reveling / Carousing</u> – Noisy partying or merrymaking. Drinking freely with noisy jollity. Clubbing or hanging out for no apparent reason but to get drunk and get in trouble. Let's stop trying to justify our behavior. Yes, Jesus' first miracle was turning water into wine at a party. You might say that contradicts the above woe, but not so. Jesus was at a wedding celebration and the wine they drank in those days was straight from the vine, which was sometimes diluted with water. It did not have the alcohol content of wine today. **Please digest this information properly. It is okay to go out and have fun, but the motives in your heart when you indulge in these activities are what make them impure.**

> *I warn you, as I did before, that those who live like this will not inherit the kingdom of God.* Galatians 5:21

<u>Gossiping, Careless Words and Giving Bad Advice</u>

God also warns us against gossiping, lying, speaking careless words and giving bad advice.

> ***But I tell you that men will have to give account on the Day of Judgment for every careless word they have spoken. For by your words you will be acquitted, and by your words you will be condemned.*** Matthew 12:36-37

Every time you open your mouth to speak, you are on trial; therefore be wise and think before you speak. When I read this Bible verse, I became so convicted that I decreased my conversation. I stopped talking so much about nothing. (I know many people would like for their spouses to read that verse.) Sometimes we are just talking to be heard and we are not saying anything. I share with you a wise comment that changed the way I communicate with others: "No one cares what you know until they know that you care." This really helped me to stop thinking that I knew everything. If you can't back up your talk with your walk, stop talking and concentrate on walking.

A fool is characterized by the many careless words he speaks. Do not make a promise to God that you do not intend to keep, because God despises this action. He would rather you not make a vow than do so and not keep your promise. (Ecclesiastes 5:2-7)

> *Whoever of you loves life and desires to see many good days, keep your tongue from evil and your lips from speaking lies. Turn from evil and do good; seek peace and pursue it.* (Psalm 34: 13-14)

"Can we all just get along?" I believe if we could not gossip or lie about each other, many of us would not have any conversation. We constantly tear each other down with our words. You know what I mean – you may be with one of your friends and talking about the other until that person comes around; then you talk about someone else who is not present. We also do this with our family members and on our jobs. Keep your tongue from negative chatter.

Bad advice is prevalent and abundant. The Word says that in the last days there will be many talkers. God warns us against giving bad advice to others. Job's friends gave him bad advice about how to handle his seemingly futile situation. Because of their bad advice, Job's friends had to bring a sacrificial offering to Job for prayer and to give unto the Lord. (Job 42:7-9) We should keep our advice to ourselves unless asked – and even then, think before we reply.

Manipulation

The spirit of manipulation is not of God. This unkind spirit has been around since the beginning when the terminator manipulated Eve to bite the fruit; then she manipulated Adam to also eat. Thus began the fall of man … until Jesus came on the scene. The spirit of manipulation has cursed women and men from generation to generation. We can manipulate just about any situation and not blink an eye. Many are so accomplished that they no longer realize they are doing it. They think, "Oh, that is just the way I am." I have a news flash for you – that is not how God intended for you to be. God did not intend for us to manipulate life for our own good, because He said that is His job.

> ***Not by (our) might nor by (our) power, but by my (God's) Spirit, says the LORD Almighty.*** Zechariah 3:6

When we go into manipulation mode, we are proving we do not trust God to fight our battles. This reveals a lack of faith in the Almighty Sovereign God.

> ***Is there anything too hard for the Lord?***
> Genesis 18:14

When we do things within our own strength, we become weary and tired, but when we allow God to handle it or guide us to the correct resolution, then we have peace.

> *Weary is the soul that has not found rest in the Lord.*
> *Tired is the body that has not followed the Holy Spirit but its flesh.*
> *Weak is the soul that has not been nourished by the Word and watered by the Holy Spirit.*
> *Heavy is the heart that has not trusted God in all things.*
> *Stressed is the mind that has not yielded and surrendered all to God.*
>
> – *"A Watchman"*

Stop trying to do God's job.

Stealing

One of the 10 commandments admonishes, "Thou shall not steal," but we continue to do it every day. We steal on our jobs when we show up late to work or take longer lunch breaks, but still report eight hours of work. We steal by reporting the incorrect amount on our travel expenditures. We steal when we take office supplies from our job to our homes without permission. We steal on our taxes when we falsely report taxable deductions. We steal from the government when we lie in order to collect food stamps, welfare, financial aid, Social Security, unemployment or any other government assistance. We steal when we make copies of music, software, CDs, DVDs or VHS movies, because we are taking money from the people who own the copyrights. We even have the nerve to steal from God.

> *"I the LORD do not change. So you, O descendants of Jacob, are not destroyed. Ever since the time of your forefathers you have turned away from my decrees and have not kept them.* ***Return to me, and I will return***

> ***to you," says the LORD Almighty. "But you ask, `How are we to return?' Will a man rob God? Yet you rob me. But you ask, `How do we rob you?' In tithes and offerings."*** Malachi 3:6-8

The sooner we face the truth, the sooner we will experience God's promises and constant flow of blessings.

Yes, New Testament saints, we are to tithe and give offerings. Tithe means a tenth part, especially as offered to God. A tenth is the least we should give. God also instructs us to give offerings and sacrificial offerings, but He will lead you by the Holy Spirit in your giving. He will guide you in who to bless, what ministry to bless and when. I can tell you the difference between an offering and a sacrificial offering. When you give and your flesh does not flinch, that is an offering, but when you give and you question whether God's hand is in your action, you have made a sacrificial offering. You will know it is from God, because there are only three sources you could have received the instructions to give. One you heard from yourself, but your selfish flesh does not want to give up the cash. Two, you heard from the enemy, but we all know that the devil does not want you funding God's missions. Therefore you must have heard from God. It might sting a little, but be obedient in your giving and God will bless you by multiplying it.

Saints, the day is upon us – we can see the distinction between the righteous and the wicked, between those who serve God and those who do not.

> *"They will be mine," says the LORD Almighty, "in the day when I make up my treasured possession. I will spare them, just as in compassion a man spares his son who serves him. And* ***you will again see the distinction between the righteous and the wicked, between those who serve God and those who do***

not." Malachi 3:17,18

We are either for God or for the devil. There is no middle ground. Stop straddling the fence.

> *Dear children, do not let anyone lead you astray. He who does what is right is righteous, just as He is righteous. He who does what is sinful is of the devil, because the devil has been sinning from the beginning. The reason the Son of God appeared was to destroy the devil's work. No one who is born of God will continue to sin, because God's seed remains in him; he cannot go on sinning, because he has been born of God. This is how we know who the children of God are and who the children of the devil are: Anyone who does not do what is right is not a child of God; nor is anyone who does not love his brother.* I John 3:7-10

> *Choose you this day who you will serve, as for me and my house we will serve the Lord.* Joshua 24:15

Disrespecting our Authority

Do you understand "submission to authority"? I misunderstood for a long time until God corrected my thinking, my heart and my actions. **Submission to authority** is essential if we are to enjoy God's promises in this life and in eternity. We think that because we are grown we can do what we want, when we want. *No, no, no,* says God. We are still under the authority of God, His Word, our government, pastors, spouses, bosses and parents. Submission is easy when the authority is a follower of God, but what happens when that is not the case? Later in this book, I will discuss what happens when the person or persons in authority are not following God's will. What should you do then?

Speaking negatively to or about your authority figure is not the answer. You must respect the one in authority in their presence and out of their presence. No more negative comments about your spouse, your boss, your pastor, your president, your parents, or any other authority figure in your life. (Acts 23:5) Start to find ways to encourage them, pray for them and lift them up – especially when they are doing wrong.

Shirking our Responsibilities

God also despises those who do not take care of their responsibilities – the people we are placed here to care for. If we do not take care of our children, spouses, parents, widows, pastors, neighbors and each other, God considers such irresponsibility to be wickedness.

> *If anyone does not provide for his relatives, and especially for his immediate family, he has denied the faith and is worse than an unbeliever.* 1 Timothy 5:8

Therefore, parents, properly care for your children. Don't just provide their needs, but give them love and attention. Also, pay your child support on time and visit your children if they are not living in your home. By the nature that God has given us, we all want to connect with the seed from which we came. The court papers are not going to matter much when we must go before God and receive His judgment. You may say you have disconnected from your child because of his mother or father. Find repentance and forgiveness in your heart. Make peace with the other parent and fulfill your responsibilities to your child and to God. You might have to be the first to say I was wrong and I am sorry. It takes courage to do that, but the Holy Spirit will be there to comfort you, because you are seeking to do God's will in your life.

Children, obey your parents. Yes, grown children, honor your mother and your father by loving and caring for them. Not out of obligation, but out of love for God and for them. You may think you are exempt from helping your parents if you had a bad relationship with them … but God knows your pain and sorrow, and He will reward your obedience and service. Don't allow the bitterness of a rocky past to block your blessings and your passage into the Promised Land. Paul said, "I forget the things which lie behind me and I press toward the mark of the higher calling."

Get your strength, patience and longsuffering from the Holy Spirit, who will comfort you. I realize that some of you are not yet at the point of relying on the Holy Spirit for comfort and wisdom. You desire an ear to listen to you and you need to hear wisdom from a human voice. If this is the case, please get in touch with your pastor, a Christian counselor or a prayer partner to discuss your hurts and emotions. But neglecting your responsibilities is not the answer.

Pride

One of the biggest woes that has plagued the church is the spirit of pride. This spirit has been so detrimental to the body of Christ that God wants me to dedicate an entire chapter on this woe. Just know that being boastful and full of pride is not of God, who hates pride with a passion – such passion that He cast an angel into hell because of it. We know that fallen angel as the devil or Satan (the terminator). In the next chapter you will understand the spirit of pride, where it came from, its characteristics, and how to break that spirit from controlling your life.

> *Every one that is proud in heart is an abomination to the LORD: ... he shall not be unpunished.* Proverbs 16:5

> *If a man thinks himself to be something, when he is nothing, he deceiveth himself.* Galatians 6:3

This life is not about you. It is about God's will being done in and through you, so **don't believe the hype.**

To All of God's Children

> *The word of the LORD came to me: "Son of man, speak to your countrymen and say to them: `When I bring the sword against a land, and the people of the land choose one of their men and make him their* ***watchman****, and he sees the sword coming against the land and blows the trumpet to warn the people, then if anyone hears the trumpet but does not take warning and the sword comes and takes his life, his blood will be on his own head.'"* Ezekiel 33:1-4

In this season, God has sent watchmen to be among you to warn you of the things to come. These men and women have a life-changing role, which is making sure they get the Word of God out to His people. Not just a word, but The Word for this season. If the watchman does not complete his task, he is responsible for the destruction of the persons whom God placed him over. As you can see, being a watchman is not something to take lightly or to play with. These people have zeal to spread God's message for this season – no matter what the cost. When I say cost, I mean not just money, but time in reading, writing, studying, teaching, preaching God's word, praying and fasting for God's people. In most cases, these are your pastors, teachers, prophets, ministers, bishops, elders and leaders. We must also beware of the false prophets. God gives us signs to look for concerning false prophets. You must check to see what is shedding off of them. Is it fleece or good fruit?

> *Watch out for false prophets. They come to you in sheep's clothing, but inwardly they are ferocious wolves. By their fruit you will recognize them.* Matthew 7:15,16a

> *But the fruit of the Spirit is love, joy, peace, patience, kindness, goodness, faithfulness, gentleness and self-control.* Galatians 5:22,23

Once you have received the Word from a watchman, the choice is yours to heed and live as Christ has commanded. If not, your destruction is on your head – not the watchman who is over you.

> *Since he heard the sound of the trumpet but did not take warning, his blood will be on his own head. If he had taken warning, he would have saved himself. But if the watchman sees the sword coming and does not blow the trumpet to warn the people and the sword comes and takes the life of one of them, that man will be taken away because of his sin, but I will hold the watchman accountable for his blood.* Ezekiel 33:5,6

To Pastors, Ministers, Leaders & Shepherds (Watchmen)

Watchmen, this message is for you. If you hear the Word of God for his people in this season and you do not speak to the people, you will be held accountable by God for their destruction. Do you want to pay that price?

> *But if the watchman sees the sword coming and does not blow the trumpet to warn the people and the sword comes and takes the life of one of them, that man will be taken away because of his sin, but I will hold the watchman accountable for his blood ...But if you do warn the wicked man to turn from his ways and he does not do so, he will die for his sin, but you will have saved yourself.* Ezekiel 33:6,9

Some watchmen are not shedding fleece or good fruit. They have been anointed by God to preach the Gospel; to heal the broken hearted; to proclaim liberty to the captives and recovery of sight to the blind; to set at liberty those who are oppressed; to proclaim the acceptable year of the Lord. *(Luke 4:18-19)* But they are lukewarm and no longer on fire for God's plan, but for their own. *"So, because you are lukewarm – neither hot nor cold – I am about to spit you out of my mouth."* Revelation 3:16

They have left their first love (serving God with all their heart, soul, mind, spirit and body) by allowing some form of sin to enter into the gates of their souls and they have become nothing but puppets in the pulpit for the enemy (the terminator). They are struggling to hear from God, because they do not want to humble themselves and acknowledge their sin by seeking God's forgiveness. Only by doing this will the strings be cut and the puppeteer (the terminator) will no longer control you. Why do you really want your church to grow numerically? Why do you really want to build a larger facility? Only you and God know the answer, which lies deep in your heart.

> *These men are blemishes at your love feasts, eating with you without the slightest qualm –* ***shepherds who feed only themselves.*** *These men are grumblers and fault-finders; they follow their own evil desires;* ***they boast about themselves and flatter others for their own advantage****.*
> *But, dear friends, remember what the apostles of our Lord Jesus Christ foretold. They said to you,* ***"In the last times there will be scoffers who will follow their own ungodly desires." These are the men who divide you, who follow mere natural instincts and do not have the Spirit****.* Jude 12,16-19

If this describes you, please go before God and restore your relationship with Him. Only then will you hear from heaven the instructions for His people in this season. (2 Chronicles 7:14) Do not allow pride to cause you to miss out on all the great things God has for you now and in eternity.

> ***No eye has seen, no ear has heard, no mind has conceived what God has prepared for those who love him.*** 1 Corinthians 2:9; Isaiah 64:4

Pastors, do not scatter the sheep of God.

> *"Woe to the shepherds who are destroying and scattering the sheep of my pasture!" declares the LORD. Therefore this is what the LORD, the God of Israel, says to the shepherds who tend my people: "Because you have scattered my flock and driven them away and have not bestowed care on them, I will bestow punishment on you for the evil you have done," declares the LORD. "I myself will gather the remnant of my flock out of all the countries where I have driven them and will bring them back to their pasture, where they will be fruitful and increase in number."* Jeremiah 23:1-3

Remember, God has entrusted you with His sheep, His Word, and His heart; therefore, take care of them and He will take care of you.

> *If you remain in me and my words remain in you, ask whatever you wish, and it will be given you. This is to my Father's glory, that you bear much fruit, showing yourselves to be my disciples.* John 15:7,8

Leaders, if you find your members leaving in droves, consider your ways. Many are being led by the Spirit of God when choosing a place of worship. They are no longer staying at a church or a particular denomination because Mother, Father and Grandma worshipped there. They are being led by God's Spirit to "Get out of the rebellious house."

> *The word of the LORD came to me: "Son of man, you are living among a rebellious people. They have eyes to*

> *see but do not see and ears to hear but do not hear, for they are a rebellious people. Therefore, son of man, pack your belongings for exile and in the daytime, as they watch, set out and go from where you are to another place. Perhaps they will understand, though they are a rebellious house."* Ezekiel 12:1-3

This is not written to bring condemnation, but to bring conviction. Do not let pride block the flow of God's promises to you and your ministry. God knows all, especially the heart and motives of man.

My sisters and brothers, God is saying to turn from your wicked ways and seek His will and purpose for your life. If you have turned from God's righteousness to the enemy's wickedness, you will die, but if you have turned from your wickedness to God's righteousness, you will surely live.

> *If a righteous man turns from his righteousness and does evil, he will die for it. And if a wicked man turns away from his wickedness and does what is just and right, he will live by doing so.* Ezekiel 33:18,19

We have been ordained by God and sent forth to prepare the people to "present themselves as living sacrifices to God." Are we leading, preparing and instructing the people according to God's Plan and for His Glory, not ours? Shepherds, the test is easy, check out the fruit that your flock is currently bearing, not past fruit, but this season's fruit.

> ***If we confess our sins, he is faithful and just and will forgive us our sins and purify us from all unrighteousness.*** I John 1:9

> *But you, dear friends, build yourselves up in your most holy faith and pray in the Holy Spirit. Keep yourselves*

in God's love as you wait for the mercy of our Lord Jesus Christ to bring you to eternal life. Jude 20,21

Words from the Heart of the Father

My heart grieves me over the ways of my people. My people perish because of lack of knowledge. Teach them my ways that they may be delivered and withstand the wiles of the devil. For in these last days I will grant peace to those who will serve me in the fullest. My love for thee is everlasting without end. I shall heal your land and deliver you to a new place. Love should always be used in all matters concerning me. Life was set before you to enjoy, but in the boundaries of my word. Let not your heart be troubled.

There is a great cry in the land and I have heard the cry of my people. I will heal their land. I will heal every crevice and broken piece of their hearts. My will shall prevail in this land.

Tell my people I am displeased in the things of this world which they have clung to. They have forgotten my ways, my precepts and my voice. They have led themselves into a wilderness that only I can deliver them from. My ways are not your way as high as the heavens are from the earth. Seek my face and I will lead you out of your wilderness into my peaceful presence. For I am the fullness thereof; the light of the world; and the comforter to a comfortless world.

In loneliness and solitude, there you will find me with my arms opened wide to embrace you and heal your wounds. There is great solitude and persecution when serving the true, wise and only living God.

I live that you may die and I died that you may live. The carnal, sinful nature, fleshy man in us must die in order for the Holy Spirit and its fruit to guide us and flourish in us.

Watchmen, tell the people that I am with them but greatly displeased in their service and disobedience. The Joy of the Lord shall come upon this city like a great rushing wind, breathing life into all the saints which desire me. I shall not hold anything good from my saints who worship me in spirit and in truth.

God will continue to anoint the leaders who have been called and are obedient. For those who are outside of my will for their lives, I will cast them down to the lake of fire.

For the wrath of the Father has been kindled against thee. (Romans 1:18) *The days will become shorter as will life. Seek the Father in heaven while you still have time. There will I be in the midst of your tears.*

Woe to those who disobey the Lord. For I know your hearts and I cannot be fooled. You shall wonder and pray for me in the last days and I will not be found. For I will raise up a new nation of people who will serve and worship me in spirit and in truth. My presence is where you are. Be still and know that I am God. Let not the sun set without communing with the Father. For I will teach you things. Jesus Christ died to bear your sins and iniquities. Turn them over to me through confession and true repentance.

As God calls Christians to a higher level, He will reveal more of Himself (spiritual things) to us, in order for us to successfully elevate. We as believers are not always ready to accept the spiritual things of God, even though we know He is capable of doing anything. Through the generations, we have lived in this carnal world so long that if we cannot consciously figure it out, we do not want to accept it as a move of God. But as the Word says, "His ways are higher than our ways." We have only scratched the surface of God's blessings and anointing for our lives.

CHAPTER FIVE

Don't Believe the Hype

The Father in heaven wants to let His people know how He despises the sin of pride. This spirit has captured the soul of many believers. Because of pride, the body of Christ (His believers) is divided. This book is a "how-to" manual. It tells you "how to" set yourself free: Simply allow the conviction of the Holy Spirit to lead you to God's truth concerning yourself and no one else.

> *Let us examine our ways and test them, and let us return to the LORD.*
> Lamentations 3:40

> *Examine yourselves to see whether you are in the faith; test yourselves. Do you not realize that Christ Jesus is in you – unless, of course, you fail the test?*
> 2 Corinthians 13:5

In the previous chapters we started the examination process, but it would not be thorough or complete if we did not examine the symptoms. Let us find the root cause of all the afflictions/ iniquities that are crippling the body of Christ. When you describe your headaches, backaches, runny nose and cough to your physician, he analyzes those symptoms; then he determines what might be triggering them. As he digs deeper into your medical history; evaluates your current condition and environment; and runs tests – then he can find the root cause for your symptoms. Your root cause might be allergies, or a virus. It is the same way with sin and iniquity. The root cause for sin is pride!

> *... Each one is tempted when, by his own evil desire, he is dragged away and enticed.* James 1:14

> *For everything in the world – the cravings of sinful man, the lust of his eyes and the boasting of what he has and does – comes not from the Father but from the world.* 1 John 2:16

God wants us to know the truth about pride so that it will not consume us. Let's go back in time to understand the origin of pride and why it is so prevalent in people. Lucifer, one of God's angels, wanted to take God's place, but God said *NO*! in a most thunderous way, casting Lucifer into the abyss (hence the name change to Satan or the devil.) This was the beginning of pride. PRIDE got Lucifer cast into hell, because he wanted to take God's place, to become the head honcho. Let's continue on with the story. Remember in the chapter, "The Terminator," that Lucifer was in the huddle and took the playbook to hell with him, so he knew about Adam, Eve and generational curses. (Exodus 34:6,7) His crafty plan was to sow the deceptive seeds of pride and manipulation into Eve.

> *"You will not surely die," the serpent said to the woman. "For God knows that when you eat of it your eyes will be opened, and* ***you will be like God, knowing good and evil.****"* Genesis 3:4,5

"You will be like God!" Can you say PRIDE! Did not Lucifer try to be like God and was cast into the abyss?

When she bit into the fruit, the sin of pride and manipulation zapped her. She in turn used manipulation to entice Adam to taste the forbidden fruit. Thus was born the generational curse of pride – the first sin to enter into the earth, and it has been with us ever since. Pride, coupled with the sin of manipulation, has cultivated a people walking in sin and justifying their wickedness by using the word of God. Wow! Was that not a crafty plan of the devil? But the story does not end there. God wants you to know the truth and the truth shall set you free. (John 8:32) If Eve had known the truth – that they were already like God, created in His image (Genesis 1:27) – she would have put the devil in his place.

My people are destroyed for lack of knowledge.
Hosea 4:6

Many of us feel we are free because of our belief in Christ Jesus, but we have not considered the enemy (the spirit of pride) that resides within us. Yes, we are free from eternal death, but our minds are still enslaved by the thinking and ways of the world. Through our conversion to Christianity, by our belief in Jesus Christ, the Holy Spirit entered us, but all the other stuff that was there did not evaporate. That is why we face a constant internal battle in our daily walk. Pride is a sin that resides in us and the sooner we understand our problems or issues, the sooner we will submit to God's purification process. If you do not think anything is broken, you will not attempt to get it fixed. This book is to illuminate – to set you free from incorrect thinking and actions so you may walk in the fullness of God's promises for your life. Most of us do not realize it is our own sin that has caused a bottleneck in the highway of God's blessings to us.

Let's take a look at some symptoms of pride:

– Do you brag and boast about your children, car, home, job, tithes, spouse, relationship with God or lifestyle? (Remember, there is a difference in bragging about you and giving a testimony. You can fool people, but God knows your heart.)
– Do you brag about your accomplishments?
– Do you boast about how much money you make?
– Do you invite people to your home just to show it off?
– Do you boast about how much better your children are doing than others? (People are doing this at an alarming rate by using their children as prize trophies. They brag about their children's accomplishments at the expense of other parents' feelings. Example ... If you know your child has great coordination and plays sports really well, why would constantly brag about your child to a parent whose child has coordination issues? We need to think before we speak. Remember, God knows the intent of your heart.)

– Do you boast about what God is doing in you spiritually? (Be careful with that – remember what happened to Joseph.)
– Do you manipulate situations so you always look good?
– Do you always want to be right? (You are never wrong and you know everything. People do not care what you know until they know that you care.)
– Do you hate to be embarrassed and will do anything to avoid it ... even lie?
– Does it pain you to apologize and take responsibility for your wrong actions? (Never accepting fault.)
– Do you look down on people who are not in the same status as you financially, spiritually, educationally or in ministry?
– Do you exalt yourself or your situation above everyone else? (You think you are better than others.)
– Can you not rejoice in others' success because of your jealousy?
– Do you not want anyone to exceed above you in status or in the spiritual things of God?
– Do you avoid asking for help even when you know you need it?
– Are you one way around your Christian friends and another around your coworkers?
– Are you nice, kind and all smiles when you are around important people, but hell on wheels when you are at home with your family? (In other words, do you have more than one face?)
– Do you feel that you deserve more than others?
– Are you only humble when it makes you look good? (False humility.)
– Do you joy in others' sorrows and grieve in their joys?
– Do you help others only to be seen by people?
– Do you seek out others' failures instead of encouraging their successes?
– Do you care what people think about you?
– Do you rely on the opinions of others to affirm you?
– Are you easily offended?

The spirit of pride will cause you to lie, cheat, steal, boast or manipulate to protect your image by saving face. Pride is the **root** sin, which causes all the other sin symptoms. **Don't believe the hype**, because this life is not about you, but about God's will being completed through you.

> ***For if a man think himself to be something, when he is nothing, he deceiveth himself.*** Galatians 6:3

It took me a while to get this, because even as I began to grow spiritually and received my call to preach God's word, I still was boasting about the changes God was doing in me. I was also bragging about the visions He was giving me. God had to quickly show me about the spirit of pride and how I had switched from pride in my worldly achievements to pride in my ministry. Please understand that the same iniquities will follow you in ministry or wherever you are, unless you confess them to God and ask Him to remove them from you. Some are thorns in the flesh to keep us from thinking we can handle it all and do not need God.

> ***To keep me from becoming conceited*** *because of these surpassingly great revelations, there was given me a thorn in my flesh, a messenger of Satan, to torment me.* 2 Corinthians 12:7

If we were perfect like Jesus and never sinned, we would think we didn't need God or the guidance of the Holy Spirit. We are to strive for perfection (spiritual maturity) like Jesus, but never think of ourselves more highly than we should. For those who humble themselves, God will exalt.

> *For everyone who exalts himself will be humbled, and he who humbles himself will be exalted.* Luke 14:11

God has to consistently remind me that "the proof is in the pudding." I do not need to brag about my accomplishments, because He will exalt me by revealing who I am in Him. Pride is a spirit that will not go down without a fight. For me, fasting and prayer helped me find humility. I preface the previous sentence with "for me" because pride may not be a temptation for some, but for many of us it is. My walk with God was strengthened when I became sincere in my humility to Him. We must face our iniquities and confess them to God ... He is just and faithful to forgive us of our sin and cleanse us of it. (I John 1:9) But the first step is acknowledging; then confessing.

The body of Christ is divided by race, religious denominations and other factions. In this season, I believe God is breaking down these barriers to reunite His people. These divisions have come about for many different reasons, but now God is revealing His truth and pride will not allow us to renege on what we have been taught or what we have taught others. If the Holy Spirit has spoken to your heart concerning religious or cultural traditions you have been taught that do not line up with the Word of God in full context – then heed the voice of the Holy Spirit by living and teaching the truth. Lives are depending on you, because the truth will set us free.

The pride of life will surely cause your demise. (Proverbs 16:18,19) By not allowing God to lead you in all things, you are saying that you know more than Him, and that is pride. (Proverbs 3:5-8)

You are presuming to take the steering wheel of life by saying, Lord sit back, relax and enjoy the ride, because I'm driving. God is the ultimate driver and navigator. We mess up every time we allow pride to operate in us and deny the Holy Spirit from navigating our lives.

I reflect on a time when God warned me of some issues that were about to arise in my home. He did not say when or exactly what but He gave us profound advice that we did not follow and the issues crept up on us. Before we knew it, we were crashing and burning because we did not rely on God. Let me share the whole story – and you will see that we must trust and rely on God even in the bad times. My spouse and I were about to experience a one-income household after living on two incomes. During a business trip, I was in my hotel room praying and studying my Bible and the Lord spoke to my heart. I know this was true wisdom imparted to me from God because it was so clear that I remembered and never had to write it down. He said that we (my spouse and I) were about to enter into a storm and to look to Him for guidance as a pilot relies on his navigational instruments to land his plane during a turbulent storm. When a pilot is flying an aircraft in stormy weather and the visibility is little or none, he must rely on his navigational instruments – not his own senses – to land safely. After hearing this Word from God, I was prepared for the storm. I watched and waited, but then thought maybe the storm had passed because we were coping okay with one salary; then a job opened up and we were back to a two-income household.

But that was not the storm. It was the wind before the real storm. I let down my guard and began to travel more with my job, leaving my spouse at home to care for our two small children. Next, I agreed with my employer to travel on Sundays, which took away my fellowship time with my church family. The enemy had me where he wanted me and was honing in on my stronghold. He had a foothold into my life – shutting me off from my support system, my family, my church family and then from the Father. I began traveling and working so much that I stopped taking my Bible with me because it was too heavy in my luggage and I did not have time to read it anyway, because when I was not working, I needed rest. This is the subtle deception of the enemy and we fall for it every time. I allowed my own selfish ambitions to pull me out of the hedge of God's protection and began to live life as I wanted; no one else mattered.

This was the storm God was referring to, but I was too weak spiritually to see the mess I had gotten myself and my family into. My kids spent more time with my spouse than with me, and when I returned from my travels, I was on the outside looking in. The Holy Spirit convicted my heart of the mess I had created, and I began to fast and pray back into God's will for my life. I returned to God and He returned to me. I know He never totally left me, but God's Glory will not dwell where there is blatant sin. I went before God and confessed my sin and He (not me but He) cleansed me of all unrighteousness. Never think because you have it all together that you do not need God's constant guidance and protection. This is where many people in the body of Christ fail: They adopt a "holier than thou" attitude by not relying on God in all things. I am no longer "The Holier than Thou Super Christian" but "The Lord Have Mercy on Me Christian."

My spouse and I came together in prayer for God's restoration in our marriage and in our relationship with Him. That night as we kneeled before God with humbled hearts, His Holy Spirit engulfed us and the tears flowed. Don't ever get too grown up for God, because if God is not using you, guess who is – "The Terminator." Don't believe the hype – you cannot handle life without God's guidance.

Within the ministry of preachers, teachers, elders and leaders, there is a jockeying for position … but God said we do not have to fight for our turn on His lap, because His lap is large enough to hold us all at one time. We either speak negatively about someone's ministry or we try to outdo others in preaching or in building the size of our congregations. This is not of God. Love one another as Christ has loved us. (I John 3:16) It is pride that keeps this Word from becoming a reality in our lives. The Word of the Lord says that pride comes before the fall.

> *Pride goes before destruction, a haughty spirit before a fall.* Proverbs 16:18

Remember – pride came before the fall of Lucifer to the abyss, and pride came before the fall of man in the garden. This is why God constantly warns us not to exalt ourselves more highly than we should, because this is a principal law of God's Word. (Luke 14:11) If you are prideful and puffed up, you are going to fall. God will not go back on His Word.

Examine where you are in life and identify the things or actions that have hindered you from achieving the next level spiritually, in your ministry, in your relationships or on your job. Most often, you will find that it was you who have hindered your advancement. Would that not be a terrible shame to get to heaven and find you were the cause of your own stagnation? God showed me how I was blocking my own blessings.

As you read this book, you will understand how your own actions and words will move you into the Promised Land or keep you in the wilderness. I don't know about you, but I want to live all of God's promises for me here on earth and in eternity. **"Don't Believe the Hype"** ... don't allow your pride to keep you from experiencing all that God desires for you. Acknowledge you have pride by asking God to forgive you of it and cleanse it from you. He is faithful and just to do so.

> *If we confess our sins, he is faithful and just and will forgive us our sins and purify us from all unrighteousness.* I John 1:9

I am so happy that I have experienced God's forgiveness and cleansing and I am no longer bound by what people think. God's approval is all that matters, because along with His approval come favor and blessings … and He sends others who will encourage you.

CHAPTER SIX

God, the Man with the Plan

Let's talk about God and who He is. If you know "the man with the plan," then you will get with THE plan … because God's plan will lead you to your purpose for existing.

Jehovah Elohim "The Eternal Creator"

Genesis 2:4-7

This is the history of the heavens and the earth when they were created, in the day that the LORD God made the earth and the heavens, before any plant of the field was in the earth and before any herbs of the field had grown. For the Lord God had not caused it to rain on the earth, and there was no man to till the ground; but a mist went up from the earth and watered the whole face of the ground. And the Lord God formed man of the dust of the ground, and breathed into his nostrils the breath of life; and man became a living being.

Since the beginning of time, God has had His own water sprinkler system for the whole earth. This chapter is all about God, His character and His awesomeness. It will help you to understand the God we serve and His limitless capabilities. Knowing about Him will draw you near to Him and the promises He has established for your life.

Jehovah Elohim, the Creator of the Heavens and the earth, the maker of all living creatures. God the Father of all and the ruler of all. God is even in control of Satan and his every move, especially when it comes to us, His children. Realize that when God wants to get you something or get you somewhere, He will move heaven and earth to make it happen. We must learn to recognize when God is on the move in our lives. He created everything; therefore we must conclude that He is in control of everything.

My training and work experience are in computer programming. The most important thing I learned as the creator of a program is that the computer is only as efficient and smart as its programmer. The computer is nothing but hardware or a bunch of parts without the software or programs to run it. God the Creator is the wisest programmer in the world. Have you surrendered to His programming, or are you still trying to program or deprogram yourself? He is the creator and controller of all things. You will be frustrated, depleted and defeated if you do not allow the Master Creator, God, to program your life. He has put a part of Him in you (**we were fashioned in His own image**), and that is why we feel guilty when we do something wrong. For all of us, these feelings occurred even before we were saved, because the Master Creator had already deposited a chip, a piece of himself within us.

Sometimes, the Creator uses a quiet space to focus on His program. When I worked on a computer program, I needed peace and quiet to fashion it the way I thought it should be. Sometimes that meant working late nights or weekends. God, of course, can work in any circumstances or environment. However, He has to shut off our contact to the people or things that are destroying us. Paul had to be imprisoned to write the most profound words of the New Testament, to escape the outside disruptions he was experiencing even while in the ministry (especially in the ministry!). It is hard to stay focused on what God is instructing us to do because of our outside disruptions, but remember: He is the Creator of it all. If He really wants you to get it done, He will shut off everything around you to get your undivided attention. God, the Creator of all things, is sovereign. He is all and over all.

Jehovah Adonai "The Lord Our Sovereign"
Genesis 15:2,8
Abram knew that all things come from God and depend on God (Sovereign). After all – he left his country and relocated his family to an undisclosed location. God said go and Abram went. He trusted God with his life and the lives of his family. Abram also trusted God's promise – to make him a father of many

nations whose offspring would be as the number of stars in the sky. He wanted God, the Sovereign Lord, to explain how that was going to happen when he did not have any sons to carry on his name and he was getting up in age. God revealed to Abram in a vision that his descendants would be enslaved (by Egypt) for four hundred years – then released along with the wealth of the land. God is Sovereign not because He predicts the future, but because He is the future. He is Alpha and Omega, the Beginning and the End. The end was created in the beginning.

God is Sovereign and He knows the end of your story. Seek His guidance as Abram did for the missing chapters. You might get only the Cliffs Notes, but it wouldn't be faith if he told you everything about your life. Trust in the sovereignty of God to guide you.

Jehovah Jiréh "The Lord will Provide"
Genesis 22:8-14
Abraham was faced with a choice – trust God or hold on to what he had. He knew that Isaac was the promised heir (seed) that would bring Abraham's promised offspring, but he did not know why God was asking him to sacrifice his promise. Has God asked you to sacrifice a promise that He has already given you? Well, Abraham was faced with either sacrificing Isaac or preparing another sacrifice, because surely God could not have meant to give up his blessing. God will stretch our faith and full trust in Him with a sacrificial offering, and when He does ... **just do it**! Because on the other side of your obedience is the promise He made you.

Abraham decided to follow God even if it meant losing his only, beloved son. Even when God is working in you by blessing you with your promise (seed), then telling you to willfully give it up, you must obey, because He is testing whether the promise means more to you than He does. It is better to obey God now and understand it later. Abraham did not fully understand why God wanted him to sacrifice His promised seed, but he obeyed God. Because of Abraham's obedience, he received again his promised seed (Isaac), another offering and the fullness of God's promise – that he would be the father of many nations and his descendants would be as the number of stars in the sky.

A wise person once told me, "If you give IT up you can have IT all." What is your IT?
What is God telling you to sacrifice in order to get what He wants for you? Is it your firstborn – meaning a ministry, book, or other precious gift He gave you? Is it your time? Is God calling you or pressing on your heart to spend more time with Him? Is it your finances? You always seem to have just enough, but never really an overflow, because He is pressing on your heart to sow into His people and ministries but you have not done so. Is it a material item that he has asked you to give up to someone and you have not obeyed Him and nothing is going right with that item? Do you even feel guilty having it? When God is pressing you to make a sacrifice, your flesh is going to cringe and deny that this request is from God. But consider this: You know that it is not Satan telling you to give to God or His children, and it is definitely not you, because remember your flesh is cringing over the thought of giving it up. You need to obey God now and understand later, because the fulfillment of His promise in your life depends on God "The Provider" coming through for you – not the promised seed. Do not put your trust and faith in the promised seed. Instead, trust God with it and He will bring the harvest, because He is Jehovah Jireh, "The Lord Will Provide."

Jehovah Nissi " The Lord is our Banner"
Exodus 17:15
Moses had not only to face an angry mob in the camp, but he also had to deal with war approaching from outside of the camp. Many leaders today are dealing with angry congregations because of impatience when waiting on God's promises to manifest (visu-

ally see and touch it). These leaders are also dealing with attacks from outside of the church. Moses realized that he could not lead these people, the descendants of Abraham, without God's guidance. Moses was getting really impatient with the murmuring and complaining from the children of Israel, so he cried out to God "What Shall I do with this people?" I believe this was done with a loud, screeching, painful cry because Moses had no choice in his calling or assignment. He had to lead the people, but he was tired of dealing with them. What do you do when you must raise a child whom you are tired of dealing with or head a household that is not allowing you to lead, or pastor a congregation that will not follow your lead? Cry out to God, our banner, leader, protector and standards, "What shall I do with this people?" Turn them over to Him. God's answer will take the pressure off of you as the leader by giving you the solution for His people. We must remember that they do not belong to us, but they belong to God and we are just shepherds over them for a short period of time. Yes, they may frustrate you from time to time, but do not let them steal your peace with God. Don't allow the sheep to get the shepherd out of peace with God or you may see the Promised Land but not be able to step into it.

Moses also had to deal with the enemies outside of the camp. He took the rod of God with him to the top of the hill and held up his hands. While his hands were aloft, Israel prevailed, but when he became tired and dropped his hands Israel began to lose. Aaron and Hur came alongside Moses to help him when it got tough. They held up his hands and Israel won the victory.

How can we today win the victory over the enemy at the gates of our homes, churches, schools and government? By praying and supporting one another. I have noticed when my prayer life is strong and I am praising God daily, the enemy cannot even come near the camp. But when I stop praying and praising, because I'm weary or tired and my guard is down (and my hands are down), the enemy begins to prevail. It takes other saints to come alongside you, realize you are having a low moment and intercede for you. Moses went up on a hill to intercede for the Israeli army. God is calling us to intercede for the body of Christ. The pettiness must stop if we are to be totally victorious over the enemy in this life. The problem with most saints is that we are so worried about ourselves, we are not sensitive to the battles of others. Sometimes we discern the problem or God reveals to us another person's issues, but instead of praying and supporting the person (lifting up their hands to get the victory), we wag our tongues to others in gossip, which helps the enemy win the battle over their plight.

I believe that God has strategically placed intercessors or prayer warriors all around the world. He knew we would limit our prayer life to the people who are closest to us. We are assigned to hold up their hands so that the whole body of Christ can be victorious. Many of us long remain in the same familiar prayer assignment. Maybe it's for a family member, church, pastor, coworker, company, CEO, national leader or a nation of people. God has put some person or persons on your mind to pray for and lift up. Be obedient, because your obedience will help them gain victory over their trials. Complete your assignment lovingly, because God loves a cheerful giver. Your sacrifice is tainted when you give it in a bad spirit. That's why God commands us to do all things in love. Oh yeah, many times they don't even know you are sacrificing yourself in fasting and prayer for them. God wants all the Glory. What you do in private, God will reward openly and in secret.

For the intercessor or prayer warrior, God nudges on our hearts in the mornings to intercede for others. This sometimes is difficult, because the Spirit is willing but the flesh is weak. I know this personally, because sometimes I do not feel like getting up to pray, but the press is so strong that I must submit to the Holy Spirit. The Holy Spirit takes over the prayer and many times you are unaware of who you are praying for, but it is better to be obedient first and understand later. God, our banner, leader, protector and standards, knows when our bodies need rest because He, the giver of life, commands us to rest. The Spirit knows who to nudge and when. If you do not answer the nudge, know that God has others who are ready to arise and pray, because His will shall be done. Trust God to guide you in your prayer life. He will lead you regarding when and what to pray for your leaders and other saints. God has the victory, but we are a part of the plan in winning that victory. Yes, God could have taken out Amalek's army with one blink, but God chose this story to illustrate to us how He uses us to fulfill His will. God protected Israel, and Amalek's people are no longer upon the earth. God, our banner, has gone before us and the enemy is no longer a threat to us. Receive God's guidance, standards and protection for your life.

Jehovah Rophé " The Lord our Healer"

Exodus 15:26

The Lord God is our healer. He delivers us from all sickness and disease. He prohibits anything or anyone from harming our bodies. You may ask why we get sick and why we have life-threatening illnesses.

> *Jesus and His disciples encountered a man who was blind at birth and the disciples asked Jesus, "Teacher, who sinned, this man or his parents, that he was born blind?" Jesus answered, "Neither this man nor his parents sinned, but that the works of God should be revealed in him."* John 9:1-3

Through the blind man's disability, the works of God were revealed. The miracle of healing takes place only when someone needs to be healed. God also promised that He would keep sickness and disease away from us. I believe that if the enemy could have his way, we would all be sick and on our way to death, but The Lord our Healer protects us from this. (Exodus 15:26)

God is also the healer of our mind, spirit and soul. When Jesus forgave the prostitute, she could not stop crying as she poured expensive perfume on His feet and wiped them with her tears and hair. She was forgiven of much; therefore she loved much. (Luke 7:36-47) Many of us whose souls have been healed by God through the forgiveness of our sins are fanatically in love with Him. We are extreme in our love for Him because He delivered us from sin, through the blood of Jesus. God, our healer, comes to heal our mind, spirit, soul and body.

Jehovah Shalom "The Lord our Peace"
Judges 6:24
The Lord our God grants us peace, which others cannot understand. God gives us peace to stand in the midst of turbulent circumstances as He calms the storms of our lives.

> *Trust in the Lord with all your heart and lean not unto your own understanding and in all your ways acknowledge Him, and He will direct your path.*
> Proverbs 3:5-6

Once I started living this beautiful Proverb, instead of just quoting it, peace became a reality in my daily life. No longer is the stress on me to know everything and do everything perfectly. It is now on Christ. I started walking by the Spirit and not by my own flesh, meaning I allowed God to make the decisions for me and I obeyed by walking out His instructions. This was a relief – not trying to figure out my life – but allowing God to show me the path, which He had set for me since the beginning of time. Allowing God to lead you in every aspect of your life brings you peace, because God's will is perfect.

The Messiah came to bring peace to the hearts of men. Accept Jesus as Lord of your life and walk by the guidance of His Holy Spirit; there you will find peace. You could go to the most beautiful place in the world and have all the money you ever desired, but that would not give you peace. It may be serene for a moment, but the peace of Christ is undying and everlasting. Try Him, because you have absolutely nothing to lose, but oh so much peace to gain.

Sometimes, because of our impatience and lack of faith, we try to solve our own problems without using the navigational system of the Holy Spirit. Once we realize we cannot fix the problem, we surrender to God. He steps in and says, *Be still and know that I am God.* This peace comes when we become mature in Christ. Spiritual maturity is a precursor to undying peace. You are no longer stressed about the little things in life, and everything becomes a little thing – even death – because you know that eternity with God awaits you. Grow up in Christ and walk in the peace which surpasses all understanding. The peace of God is available to all His children, if we would just receive it.

> *Let the peace of Christ rule in your hearts, since as members of one body you were called to peace. And be thankful.* Colossians 3:15

Jehovah Tsidkeenu "The Lord our Righteousness"
Jeremiah 23:6; 33:16
God has provided righteousness for His children through the blood of Jesus Christ, "the branch sprout from David's line." Once sin was committed in the garden by Adam, God had to put the plan in motion to restore His chosen seed to righteousness. The plan was there since the beginning of time, but after the fall of man, the plan to raise Christ was executed. God knew that man would fall in sin. He knew what happened in the Garden of Eden before it happened. He knew that we would need a path of restoration before the beginning of the earth. His plan was to have righteous children and He would do what it took to restore our righteousness. Once we accepted Jesus into our hearts as Lord of our lives, then we became the righteousness of God through Christ Jesus. Once we accept God's clothing of

righteousness, we can operate and function in this world at a greater level than the wicked, but first we must accept and receive who we really are in Christ Jesus. The righteousness of God cannot be bought, bartered or traded. It was paid for by the blood of Jesus Christ when He died on the cross for the remission of our sin. Jesus paid the price for our righteousness and we must begin to walk in it. Now beware, because when you walk in your righteousness, people (saints and non-saints) will perceive it as arrogance or conceit. But we know not to get puffed up and prideful ("Don't Believe the Hype"). This righteousness dictates to believer that they can do all things through Christ (the anointing), which strengthens them. Fear is no longer an option. Stress is no longer a factor in their lives. Offenses from others are like water flowing off a duck's back. Walking in victory over the enemy is reality for the righteous. Walking in obedience to God is no longer a struggle, but a privilege. Getting all the promises that God gives to the righteous becomes a lifestyle and not a ritualistic challenge. Receiving the righteousness of God through Christ Jesus promises a victorious life with abundant peace and love. Take your place, saints, and lay claim to your new robe of righteousness in Christ Jesus. Once you know that you know, you will not settle for less, because you have experienced the best, the righteousness of God through Jesus the Christ.

Jehovah Mekaddishkem "The Lord our Sanctifier"

Exodus 31:13; Leviticus 20:8, 21:8

God makes us holy (sanctified) through the power of the Holy Spirit, hence the name "Holy Spirit." Yes, there are other spirits that are not of God, but the Holy Spirit is the only Spirit that can make us Holy. If you read the chapter, "Christian in Drag," you know that you cannot receive the Holy Spirit of God until you believe in your heart that Jesus is Lord and that God raised Him from the dead. Once the Holy Spirit indwells us, God begins to lead us to change (repentance) from the inside out. This change is an ongoing process. God changes us from Glory to Glory by getting us to the level of perfection (spiritual maturity) in Christ Jesus. We reach perfection once we become mature in Christ, but the Holy Spirit is always at work in us, because He is there to lead, comfort, protect, intercede and teach us. We must understand that we cannot change ourselves, because it will not work. Only through God's Spirit can we become Holy or Sanctified. We are to examine ourselves (Lamentations 3:40), by asking the Holy Spirit to reveal the things in us and about us that are not of God, and once that is done, ask for the Holy Spirit's guidance to lead us in getting cleaned up. The Holy Spirit will sometimes strip a sinful desire totally away from us without our intervention and sometimes He will give us instructions on what to do to remove the sin from our life, but ultimately we must obey the Spirit of God for the change to take place. Only God by His Spirit can purify us. Accept Jesus, and allow the Holy Spirit to purify you.

Jehovah Saboath "The Lord of Hosts"/ El Shaddai "The Lord Almighty"

> *Year after year this man went up from his town to worship and sacrifice to the LORD Almighty at Shiloh, where Hophni and Phinehas, the two sons of Eli, were priests of the LORD.* I Samuel 1:3
>
> *I appeared to Abraham, to Isaac and to Jacob as God Almighty, but by my name the LORD I did not make myself known to them.* Exodus 6:3

God is God all by Himself and He does not need our help to rotate the earth or keep the stars from falling or keep the sun at the right distance from the planets so they will not burn up. If we better understand who God really is and how awesome He is, then we will stop playing games with Him and start to truly reverence Him – not just on Sundays. Don't think you are fooling God, because He knows everything. He is waiting for you to come clean with Him. Hannah, the mother of Samuel, was unable to have children. She desired children so desperately that she prayed to God for a child and promised to give Him to God when He was born. In those days, having a male child was very important to people. It dictated your standing in the community. People mocked and looked down on women who could not have children. Hannah was mocked and criticized much by her rival (the other woman), but little did the rival know that Hannah had God Almighty, "The Lord of Hosts," on her side. Hannah prayed a gut wrenching prayer to God – so powerful that her lips were moving, but no sound proceeded from her mouth. The priest Eli saw her and thought she was drunk, but God heard her heart and felt her spirit. Then Eli prayed that God would grant her request. God blessed Hannah with a son, Samuel, and she dedicated him to God as an offering of thanksgiving. This was not your normal church service dedication – she literally gave him over to God by allowing him to live with the priest, Eli, and be trained by him. She kept her promise to God and even gave a thanksgiving offering to Him. Because of her dedication to God, Hannah was blessed with three more sons and two daughters. Also, Samuel, her firstborn, became one of the greatest and most respected prophets of all Israel. Hannah's prayer of thanksgiving (I Samuel 2:1-10) is a tribute to the Lord of Hosts, God Almighty, who can take a barren women and heal her womb to bear not just any child, but a child who was used mightily by God. Do you really know who God is?

Jehovah Shammah "The Lord is Present"

Ezekiel 48:35

Ezekiel was a prophet of God who was instructed by God on how the city of Jerusalem and the temple would be rebuilt. Ezekiel was first sent to warn the people of their disobedience. Then he was asked to record the dimensions of the temple and the division of the land in the city. Ezekiel was given the grievous task of seeing the destruction of the Israelites because of their disobedience, but he also received a vision from God on the restoration of God's Holy City. The sacred land was for the chosen people and was never to be sold or given away. The people were told that this is the place where God is present. As we know, God is omnipresent and He can be in all places at one time – but sometimes, His presence is felt stronger in certain places. This Holy place was where the Israelites came to worship in the temple of God – in a city that was divided by gate entrances that were named according to the 12 tribes of Israel. This was and still is a significant location for the Jews, and it is still being fought over. We as saints of God know that He is present everywhere we go, because His Holy Spirit dwells in us (the temples of God).

> *Don't you know that you yourselves are God's temple and that God's Spirit lives in you? If anyone destroys God's temple, God will destroy him, for God's temple is sacred, and you are that temple.* (1 Corinthians 3:6,17)

> *Those whom I love I rebuke and discipline. So be earnest, and repent. Here I am! I stand at the door and knock.* ***If anyone hears my voice and opens the door, I will come in*** *and eat with him, and he with* me. (Revelations 3:19,20)

Have you opened the door of your heart and allowed God's presence to come in to feed your spirit? The Glory cloud did not follow but it led the children of Israel. Is God's presence leading you?

Jehovah Elyon "The Lord Most High"

Psalm 7:17; 47:2; 97:9

Pagans were introduced into the children of Israel because the king permitted marriages to women outside the Israeli race. These women from other countries brought with them their pagan gods and religious traditions. The psalmist indicates that the God of Israel is higher than any other god.

For you, O Lord, are the Most High over all the earth; you are exalted far above all gods. Psalm 97:9

God knows He is the great I AM and there are no other gods higher. We also know that God is the only true and wise God, the Alpha and Omega, the beginning and the end. Then why did God declare in the first and second commandments:

You shall have no other gods before me. You shall not make for yourself an idol in the form of anything in heaven above or on the earth beneath or in the waters below. You shall not bow down to them or worship them; for I, the Lord your God, am a jealous God, punishing the children for the sin of the fathers to the third and fourth generation of those who hate me, but showing love to a thousand generations of those who love me and keep my commandments. Exodus 20:3-6

Is it possible that God already knew this would be a problem with the children of Israel and with us today? These two commandments refer to idolatry, to putting someone or something before God in our lives. Today we have many gods that we consider before serving and worshipping God – our careers, homes, money, children, ministries, favorite preacher and sometimes other gods such as Allah, the god of Ishmael, or the virgin Mary, mother of Jesus. God said to give honor to whom honor is due but he never said to bow down and worship another human, dead or alive. We worship Jesus, because He is the Messiah and God ordained Him as the Son of God, and the Word made flesh. God gave Jesus the authority to be worshipped. Matthew 2:11; Romans 14:11,12; Philippians 2:10,11

What or who has become your idol? Where do you spend most of your time and serving whom? Are we really serving God as "The Most High" or does He take a back seat to all the other things and people who occupy our lives? When God is ready to get your attention, He will turn off everything and everyone around you. Don't let Him get your attention in that manner, because trust me, it is not fun to be put in "time out" by God. Start to serve Him with all your heart, mind, body and soul as "The Lord Most High," worthy of all your praise.

Jehovah Rohi "The Lord, My Shepherd"
Psalm 23:1
The Lord is my Shepherd, I shall not be in want. Are you wanting for anything – such as finances, food, shelter, peace, joy, love or happiness? If so, who is your shepherd? If the Lord is your Shepherd and you are following His lead, you should not want for anything. He will grant you the desires of your heart, if you delight yourself in Him. (Psalm 37:4) God leads His sheep to a place of peace, tranquility and abundance. When I was my shepherd and allowed the pressures of society to also become my shepherds, I stayed in want and was unfulfilled. But when I allowed self to die by submitting to the leadership of the true Shepherd, I did not want for anything and peace abounded within me. The only time I am in a non-peaceful state is when God has told me to do something and I have not done it. Talk about torment – try knowing God and the power of His resurrection, then hearing a command from Him that you do not obey. You will not rest until it is done.

> *We proclaim to you what we have seen and heard, so that you also may have fellowship with us. As our fellowship is with the Father and with his Son, Jesus Christ.* ***We write this to make our joy complete.***
> I John 1:3-4

John's joy would not have been complete if he had ignored God's instructions. John was compelled to write what he was told, because he truly knew Jesus. I had to write this book or I would have been tormented by the sin of omission – by not doing what God had instructed me to do.

If God is truly your Shepherd, then you shall not be in want because He will lead you to greener pastures. Are you following the Lord, your Shepherd, or are you straying from the fold and content with gnawing on dry pastures? God, "The Good Shepherd" is always leading His sheep to greater and greener pastures. Trust God, "The Lord Your Shepherd," by following His lead.

> *Commit your way to the LORD;* ***trust in him*** *and he will do this: He will make your righteousness shine like the dawn, the justice of your cause like the noonday sun.*
> Psalm 37:5,6

Psalm 23

The ***LORD is my shepherd****, I shall not be in want.*
He makes me lie down in green pastures,
He leads me beside quiet waters,
He restores my soul.
He guides me in paths of righteousness
for His name's sake.
Even though I walk
through the valley of the shadow of death,
I will fear no evil,
for you are with me;
your rod and your staff,
they comfort me.
You prepare a table before me
in the presence of my enemies.
You anoint my head with oil;
my cup overflows.
Surely goodness and love will follow me
all the days of my life,
and I will dwell in the house of the LORD
forever.

Jehovah Hoseenu "The Lord Our Maker"

Psalm 95:6

We are wonderfully and fearfully made by God. Even before we were born, God knew every detail about us. (Psalm 139:14-16) We are intricately formed and fashioned by God, so much so that He has numbered the hairs on our head. (Matthew 10:30) We are so special to God that he made us a little lower than Him (Elohim). (Psalm 8:3-5) Once we know how important we are to Him and how much he loves us, then we will begin to appreciate ourselves more. This is for those saints who have low self-esteem: God has made you in His image. Get up off your bed of self-pity and out of your cave of depression, because "The Lord, Your Maker" has a plan for your life. Do not allow fear to rule your life, because if God is for you, then no one can come against you. (Romans 8:31) They may try, but God has you covered. (Psalm 91)

> *Come, let us bow down in worship, let us kneel before the Lord our Maker; for he is our God and we are the people of his pasture, the flock under his care.* Psalm 95:6

Jehovah Eloheenu "The Lord Our God"

Psalm 99:5, 8,9

> *Exalt the Lord our God and worship at His holy mountain, for the Lord our God is holy.*

> "Our God is an awesome God.
> He reigns from heaven above,
> with wisdom power and love.
> Our God is an awesome God."

These are words to one of my favorite songs, because they praise God and speak to how awesome He is. God inhabits the praises of His people. Praising God is the key that unlocks the flow of His promises in our lives. Many times we sing songs that do not praise God, but instead dwell on our past struggles, but when we begin to sing praise to God He shows up in the midst of our praise. The Lord Our God is awesome and should be reverenced and praised as such. Begin to praise "The Lord Our God," and see what your praise will manifest. *Holy, Holy, Holy Lord God Almighty, who was and is and is to come.* Revelation 4:8

Jehovah Elokehu "The Lord Thy God"

Exodus 20:2, 5, 7

> *I am* ***the Lord Thy God*** *... You shall not bow down to or worship idols; for I,* ***the Lord Thy God,*** *am a jealous God ... You shall not misuse the name of* ***the Lord Thy God*** *...*

How much does God really mean to you and how well do you treat your relationship with the Father? Do you take Him for granted by knowing He is always there, but never (or maybe only sometimes) acknowledging Him? Do you respect and honor His name or do you sling it around like a preposition or a conjunction? Do you spend time with Him or are you too caught up in your church committee meetings, your religious traditions? Do you have a relationship with God or are you worshipping your religion? How well do you really reverence the Lord Your God? Yes, God's heart hurts and grieves when we do not spend time with Him, then take his mercy and grace for granted. Like any father, He wants to be thanked and appreciated. The Word says to enter His gates with thanksgiving and His courts with praise. (Psalm 100:4) Many of us cannot get to the Promises of God for our lives, because we can't get past the gates. We do not thank or praise Him enough. I do not know of any father who does not like love, praise and thanks for the things he does for his children. God created us to commune with Him – not just talk about Him in passing. He desires your undivided attention, respect, honor, praise and thanksgiving. Consider taking some time to give "The Lord Thy God" the respect, love, honor and appreciation He deserves. "The Lord Thy God" desires (requires) all of you – not just the morsels of your life that you have been giving to Him.

Jehovah Elohay "The Lord My God"
Zechariah 14:5

> *... Then "The Lord My God" will come and all the holy ones with Him.*

There is coming a time when "The Lord My God" will return and reign over all the earth. He will bring with Him to the battle of Megiddo the holy ones. (Revelation 19:14) The enemy will be defeated and removed from the heavens and the earth forever. There will be a new heaven and a new earth. Jesus will establish His kingdom forever. Now is the time to know for sure if your name is in the Lamb's Book of Life. Do you really know Jesus or have you simply *attended* church all your life? Check out the chapter, "Christian in Drag," if you are still not sure of your salvation. Every prophecy in God's word will be fulfilled and Jesus' return is no exception. God said it and it will come to pass. "The Lord My God" is on His way back with the holy ones who are mounting up in preparation for battle and His glorious return. Are you ready?

> *Then I saw* ***a new heaven and a new earth, for the first heaven and the first earth had passed away,*** *and there was no longer any sea. I saw the Holy City, the new Jerusalem, coming down out of heaven from God, prepared as a bride beautifully dressed for her husband. And I heard a loud voice from the throne saying, "Now the dwelling of God is with men, and he will live with them. They will be his people, and God himself will be with them and be their God. He will wipe every tear from their eyes. There will be no more death or mourning or crying or pain, for the old order of things has passed away."*

He who was seated on the throne said, "I am making everything new!" Then he said, "Write this down, for these words are trustworthy and true."

He said to me: "It is done. I am the Alpha and the Omega, the Beginning and the End. To him who is thirsty I will give to drink without cost from the spring of the water of life. He who overcomes will inherit all this, and I will be his God and he will be my son. But the cowardly, the unbelieving, the vile, the murderers, the sexually immoral, those who practice magic arts, the idolaters and all liars – their place will be in the fiery lake of burning sulfur. This is the second death."
Revelation 21:1-8

Your assignment for this chapter is on the following page. Fill in "The Alphabet of Praise and Thanksgiving" chart according to who God is to you and what you are thankful for. This chart is also helpful during your time of prayer.

The Alphabet of Praise and Thanksgiving

God you are:

A	Awesome, Almighty, Alive . . .	N	
B		O	
C		P	
D		Q	
E		R	
F		S	
G		T	
H		U	
I		V	
J		W	
K		X	
L		Y	
M		Z	

God we thank you for:

A	Air, Autumn, Apples . . .	N	
B		O	
C		P	
D		Q	
E		R	
F		S	
G		T	
H		U	
I		V	
J		W	
K		X	
L		Y	
M		Z	

Chapter Seven

Restoration

God wants His people to return to Him instead of suffering the consequences of living sinful lives by perpetrating a fraud ("Christian in Drag"). If you saw yourself or some characteristics of yourself in the previous chapters, then now is the time to get it right with God. This chapter consists of a 12-step process that will lead you back to God. Many of us make the New Year's resolution, "I'm going to get closer to God," and here are the steps on how you can do that. Remember – no pain, no gain – but the Holy Spirit will be there to guide and comfort you each step of the way. Restoration requires sincere repentance that hurts the heart, grieves the spirit and cleanses the soul.

God wants His people to return to Him by restoring a right relationship with Him. God revealed a vision to me concerning His saints. He showed me His arms stretched out wide like a father waiting to embrace his children; then He embraced all of His children at once and lifted us to a higher level. This was not the rapture; it happened here on earth. He then explained that in the near future – now – there will be a separation between the righteous and the wicked. The commingling of the two groups will cease. There will be an immediate distinction between the righteous and the wicked. God is lifting His saints to higher ground in every aspect of life, but you must abide in Him and He in you for this elevation to take place. You must be of the righteous and not the wicked. Can you accept Jesus as Lord of your life and still be considered wicked?

> *Then those who feared the LORD talked with each other, and the LORD listened and heard. A scroll of remembrance was written in his presence concerning those who feared the LORD and honored his name. "They will be mine," says the LORD Almighty, "in the day when I make up my treasured possession I will spare them, just as in compassion a man spares his son who serves him. And you will again see the distinction between the righteous and the wicked, between those*

> *who serve God and those who do not."*
> Malachi 3:16-18

This is a prophecy given by Malachi that is now being fulfilled. These persons who are considered God's treasured possession feared the LORD, honored His name and served Him. Are you honoring God with your lifestyle? Are you serving Him with your time, treasures, and spiritual gifts? I am not talking about just attending church once or twice a week and giving your tithes in a legalistic sense. I am asking if you have a relationship with God that means you get your day-to-day instructions from the Holy Spirit.

> *Trust in the LORD with all your heart and lean not on your own understanding; in all your ways acknowledge him, and he will make your paths straight.*
> Proverbs 3:5, 6

Do not get overwhelmed. Remember, this is a "how-to" manual and it contains step-by-step instructions that will lead you, with the Holy Spirit's guidance, back to God. Open your mind, but most importantly, open your heart to the Holy Spirit's process of transforming you from Glory to Glory by maturing you into the person God truly desires you to be.

> *If my people, who are called by my name, will humble themselves and pray and seek my face and turn from their wicked ways, then will I hear from heaven and will forgive their sin and will heal their land. Now my eyes will be open and my ears attentive to the prayers offered in this place.* 2 Chronicles 7:14 -15

In this Bible verse, Solomon had completed the construction of the temple and He was interceding – praying – for the children of Israel. (2 Chronicles 6) He wanted God to bless them. God spoke to him and stated these four instructions, which would lead God's people to a restored relationship with Him. Then He would hear their prayer, forgive their sin, and heal their land. If you take notice, Solomon could not perform this process for them; he could only give them God's instructions. I can only reveal to you what God took me through in order to write this book. No one can go through this process for you. You must be processed in order to enter into the Promised Land of God.

Humble Yourself (Humiliation)

1. Humble yourself before God by acknowledging that you have sin in your life. Many of us feel as if we have arrived when we accept Jesus Christ as Lord and Savior. Then we sit in the pew every Sunday, but sin all week long while judging and condemning others. But God says if you say you have no sin then you make Him into a liar.

> *When they kept on questioning him, he straightened up and said to them,* ***"If any one of you is without sin, let him be the first to throw a stone at her."***
> John 8:7
>
> ***If we claim to be without sin, we deceive ourselves and the truth is not in us.*** *If we confess our sins, he is faithful and just and will forgive us our sins and purify us from all unrighteousness.* ***If we claim we have not sinned, we make him out to be a liar and his word has no place in our lives.*** 1 John 1: 8-10

Stop trying to fool God, because He knows everything. He knows your thoughts even before you think them. Humble yourself before God Almighty, who created the heavens and the earth, by admitting your sins to Him. I asked God the question, "Lord I thought you said you died for our past, present and future sins." The Lord replied, "I did, but you have to give them to me." We hold our sin by repeating the same sin, or harboring a past sin, or wallowing in guilt and condemnation. We MUST confess our sin to God, then He is faithful and just to forgive us and cleanse us of all unrighteousness. This is the process of purification, refining, purging, pruning, circumcision of the heart or coming clean with God. It is time we stop just tidying up, and seriously embark on an internal spring-cleaning. Think about it – if we did not have to confess our sin to God, then why would all the saved people need to go and be judged by God? We should be able to walk into heaven, bow at the Master's feet and confess Him as Lord, but no –there is a judgment day for the saints also.

> *For we must all appear before the judgment seat of Christ, that each one may receive what is due him for the things done while in the body, whether good or bad.*
> 2 Corinthians 5:10

> *Now all has been heard; here is the conclusion of the matter: Fear God and keep his commandments, for this is the whole duty of man.* ***For God will bring every deed into judgment, including every hidden thing, whether it is good or evil.*** Ecclesiastes 12:13,14

---

2. Ask God through the power of the Holy Spirit to reveal the things in you that are not of Him. List your sins so that you will not leave anything out. I chose to list the things the Holy Spirit was revealing to me about myself, so that I would not miss anything, but God knows your heart and if a situation is not straight with Him, the Holy Spirit will remind you of it.

> *Let us examine our ways and test them, and let us return to the LORD.*
> Lamentations 3:40

> *A man ought to examine himself before he eats of the*

> *bread and drinks of the cup. For anyone who eats and drinks without recognizing the body of the Lord eats and drinks judgment on himself.*
> 1 Corinthians 11:28-29

> *Examine yourselves to see whether you are in the faith; test yourselves. Do you not realize that Christ Jesus is in you – unless, of course, you fail the test?*
> 2 Corinthians 13:5

The Holy Spirit is going to reveal some situations that God would like for you to rectify, because it is on the books and judgment day is coming. These situations might be in your distant past or in your present. Do not disregard them, because they are coming to your mind and heart for a reason. This is where most people get stuck in the blame game, depression, pleading the victim, or straight-out denial. Do not let the enemy fool you with these tactics. Listen to the Holy Spirit and take your medicine, because only then will you begin to get spiritually well. Also, don't forget the issues in the previous chapters that you highlighted or underscored. Remember – you may want to write these issues down, because you do not want to leave anything out when going to the next step. This is where God may reveal the truth about you and it may sting a little. For those who have not done this self-examination in a while there is going to be much junk in your trunk – so take a break and allow God to minister to you during this process.

Prayer (Communication)

Next, God desires for us to communicate with Him and others by sincerely seeking **forgiveness**.

3. Sincerely ask God for forgiveness of your sins.

> *If we confess our sins, he is faithful and just and will*

forgive us our sins and purify us from all unrighteousness. 1 John 1:9

If I regard iniquity in my heart, the Lord will not hear me. Psalm 66:18

But your iniquities have separated between you and your God, and your sins have hid [his] face from you, that he will not hear. Isaiah 59:2

Many of our prayers and promises are being block because of the sin in our lives. The Father is waiting with open arms to forgive you. He does not want any one of His children to perish.

These next two steps will take humiliation and strength from the Holy Spirit, because you are going to have to forgive people who have done terrible things to you. You can do this 12-step process only by the power of the Holy Spirit. If you are finding these steps difficult, then pray to God for help, because you must forgive others. Not just in lip service, but in your heart, because Jesus said if you do not forgive others, then God the Father cannot forgive you. (Mark 11:25,26) Remember, "Don't Believe the Hype." Put your pride aside.

4. Sincerely seek forgiveness from those you have wronged.

5. Sincerely forgive those who have wronged you.

Put on therefore, as the elect of God, holy and beloved, bowels of mercies, kindness, humbleness of mind, meekness, longsuffering; Forbearing one another, and forgiving one another, if any man have a quarrel against any: even as Christ forgave you, so also [do] ye. Colossians 3:12-13

Let all bitterness, and wrath, and anger, and clamour, and evil speaking, be put away from you, with all malice: And be ye kind one to another, tenderhearted, forgiving one another, even as God for Christ's sake hath forgiven you. Ephesians 4:31-32

Judge not, and ye shall not be judged: condemn not, and ye shall not be condemned: forgive, and ye shall be forgiven. Luke 6:37

And when ye stand praying, forgive, if ye have ought against any: that your Father also which is in heaven may forgive you your trespasses. But if ye do not forgive, neither will your Father which is in heaven forgive your trespasses. Mark 11:25-26

Then came Peter to him, and said, Lord, how often shall my brother sin against me, and I forgive him? Till seven times? Jesus saith unto him, I say not unto thee, until seven times: but, until seventy times seven. Matthew 18:21-35

---

6. Sincerely forgive yourself.

Now you must, I repeat you must, forgive yourself. Do not walk around in shame or in condemnation. Remember – the terminator was counting on that tactic to work and that is why he started after you at such a young age. Don't allow the enemy to steal your joy by self-inflicted condemnation. Stop carrying around dead weight (past issues) that is slowing down your stride towards God's destiny for your life. If God has forgiven you, then you should be able to forgive yourself, because nothing can separate you from the love of God.

Do not be afraid; you will not suffer shame. Do not fear disgrace; you will not be humiliated. You will forget the shame of your youth and remember no more the reproach of your widowhood. For your Maker is your husband – the LORD Almighty is his name – the Holy One of Israel is your Redeemer; he is called the God of all the earth. Isaiah 54:4,5

There is therefore now no condemnation to them which are in Christ Jesus, who walk not after the flesh, but after the Spirit. Romans 8:1

For I am persuaded, that neither death, nor life, nor angels, nor principalities, nor powers, nor things present, nor things to come, nor height, nor depth, nor any other creature, shall be able to separate us from the love of God, which is in Christ Jesus our Lord.
Romans 8:38-39

You must use much discernment and wisdom from God concerning this next step to protect your reputation and dignity. Your confession may be to the person or persons you have hurt in the past. Please, sir, and please, ma'am, be led by God to the right person (a righteous person), the right time and the right place, to make your confession, because at the wrong time, in the wrong place or to the wrong person could cause more harm than good. Confession to others brings a spirit of humiliation and is good for the soul. It also fosters accountability. Not everything needs to be confessed to another, so do not do the next step until you are led by the Holy Spirit.

7. Confess your sins one to another.

Confess your faults one to another, and pray one for another, that ye may be healed. The effectual fervent prayer of a righteous man availeth much. James 5:16

King David committed sin before God by committing adultery with Bathsheba and killing her husband after she got pregnant during the affair. Then he took her as his wife and they gave birth to the child who was conceived during the affair. You know the story – the child took sick and died. The prophet Nathan informed David that God was unhappy with his sin. David fasted and prayed to God for forgiveness by asking God to restore to him the joy of His salvation. God restored David by allowing Bathsheba to give birth to the wisest King who ever lived – King Solomon. Also, King Solomon was given favor by God to build the temple, and God allowed Jesus, our Lord and Savior, to come through the lineage of King David. God had mercy on King David and restored his joy.

God will do the same for you. Many of us have lost the joy of God's salvation because of heavy work loads, family life, church work, social clubs, bad relationships, sinful lifestyles, lack of prayer, lack of studying God's Word or not sensing God's presence in our lives. I was at a crossroad in my life when God took me through this process. It took me two and one half years – because I did not fully understand what was happening. As He guided me through victoriously, He pressed upon my heart to write this book to help others press into the presence of God and experience all the promises He has for us. I was tired of religious traditions. I wanted to feel God's presence. I wanted more of Him. I got to this stage and cried out to the Lord, "RESTORE UNTO ME THE JOY OF YOUR SALVATION!"

8. Pray that God would restore to you the JOY OF HIS SALVATION. Psalm 51

Seek My Face (Adoration)

God desires for us to seek Him. I have always had this burning desire for more and for the best of everything in life. When I reached one milestone, I was not satisfied and wanted more. This was happening in every area of my life except my relationship with God. Neither my career, my family, nor my material things could give me everything I desired. I finally cried out to God, why did you put the zealous desire in me to want more? If this is not of you, God, take it away. God replied to me by saying, *I put the desire to want more in all of my children, in some more than others, but this desire was not meant for more of the world, but for more of me.* That was a life-changing revelation for me and I started channeling that desire to wanting more of God than wanting status and things of this world. It has radically changed my life and my relationship with God. I challenge you to seek God's face. The next step explains what it means to seek His face.

---

9. Seek God's destiny and purpose for your life. Ask God, **"Lord what would you have me do? What is your will for my life?"** God is standing by, waiting for you to ask that question. In asking that question, you are seeking His divine (perfect) guidance for your life. We must understand that our life is like a book in which we are in the middle and God knows the end of the story. If a book was not published and you had the privilege of reading the first few chapters, then wanted to know about the ending, where would you go to get that information? From the author, of course, because only he knows the end to his story. God is the author and finisher of our faith and our lives are already completed in heaven. God knows the end of the story. That is why the prayer in the book of Matthew states, "Thy will be done on earth as it is in heaven." Because the story is finished in heaven, and we are seeking the manifestation of God's will for our lives here on earth.

But seek ye first the kingdom of God, and his righteousness; and all these things shall be added unto you.
Matthew 6:33

God knew you before you were placed in your mother's womb. He had your destiny mapped out, but the terminator stepped in before the full manifestation of God's will for your life. But you are still on target, because everything that the enemy meant for evil, God will use for good. Know that you have a specific assignment, and God, more than anyone, wants you to get that assignment and proceed to your destiny, because many are awaiting your arrival. If I had not come to myself, like the prodigal son did, then this book, which is one of my assignments, would not be in your hands, helping you get to your destiny in Christ Jesus. Glory be to the Father in heaven who has mercy on whom He chooses. Just know without a shadow of a doubt that you have a destiny, and God wants your undivided attention to get you there quickly.

For whom ***he did foreknow, he also did predestinate*** *to be conformed to the image of his Son, that he might be the firstborn among many brethren. Moreover whom* ***he did predestinate, them he also called****: and whom he called, them he also justified: and whom he justified, them he also glorified.* Romans 8:29,30

"Before I formed you in the womb I knew you, before you were born I set you apart; I appointed you as a prophet to the nations." Jeremiah 1:5

The next step is very important, because many of us at this point begin to feel the call on our lives but try to execute that call without God's wisdom. Do not skip the step of seeking God's divine wisdom. I began to pray for God's divine wisdom because I wanted to know the truth and to walk in the calling that God was sending me. I did not want to go back to sleeping with the swine as the prodigal son did; therefore I had to seek God's wisdom to make decisions based on His guidance. When I asked for wisdom, God opened up the windows of heaven and poured out such abundant wisdom that I did not have enough room to receive it. I began to read the Bible and the words jumped off the pages into my heart. I vigorously studied God's Word and filled many journals. I could not get enough of His wisdom. When God's wisdom is poured out on you, your discernment increases and you sense God's Holy Spirit warning you of possible danger. It is similar to Spiderman when he senses danger – his spidey sense tingles to warn him of impending peril. That's what happens when you get closer to God and receive His wisdom. The Holy Spirit warns you of things to come to protect you from emotional, physical, mental or spiritual pitfalls.

10. Ask God for His divine wisdom. God desires for us to ask for His wisdom. He does not want us to be ignorant to the things that pertain to Him.

> *My people are destroyed from lack of knowledge.*
> Hosea 4:6

> *If any of you lacks wisdom, he should ask God, who gives generously to all without finding fault, and it will be given to him.* James 1:5

> *For you were once darkness, but now you are light in the Lord. Live as children of light (for the fruit of the light consists in all goodness, righteousness and truth) and* ***find out what pleases the Lord.***
> Ephesians 5:8-10

Turn from their wicked ways (Adaptation)

> ***No one who is born of God will continue to sin,***
> ***because God's seed remains in him;***
> ***he cannot go on sinning, because he has been born***
> ***of God.*** I John 3:7-10

11. Turn away from the ways of the world and do what God has called you to do. This might be a small step at first, like reading a particular book of the Bible, tithing, or increasing your offering. Then it might intensify to greater tasks that God will ask you to complete. He is testing to see if He can trust you in the little things; then He will make you ruler over much more. (Matthew 25:21&23) Tithes and offering are important in getting closer (returning) to God.

> *"Return to me, and I will return to you," says the*
> *LORD Almighty. But you ask, 'How are we to return?'*
> *"Will a man rob God? Yet you rob me." But you ask,*
> *'How do we rob you?' "In tithes and offerings. You are*
> *under a curse – the whole nation of you – because you*
> *are robbing me."* Malachi 3:6-9

God knew in this season how we would regard money; therefore He knew that if we would trust Him with our money, we would trust Him with everything. Get past the money issue because it is not yours; it belongs to God. Don't let your idolatry of money block the fulfillment of God's promises for your life. Trust God with your finances.

After you get your instructions from God, perform them … because Christianity is a working faith. If you have no works, your faith is dead. I am not talking about church works, I am referring to what God has specifically asked you to execute. You should have zeal to serve God and His people in some way. If you do not have zeal, then reread "Christian in Drag," because your faith should spark and produce works.

> *But wilt thou know, O vain man, that faith without works is dead?* James 2:20

> ***For as the body without the spirit is dead, so faith without works is dead also.***
> James 2:26

> ***Now faith is the substance of things hoped for, the evidence of things not seen.*** Hebrews 11:1

Faith and works go hand in hand. Faith without works is a dead faith and works without faith are like filthy rags to God. Please understand that God is holding us accountable for the sins we commit and the works we omit. Many people treat salvation like getting a "D" in a tough class. They rejoice because they pass the class and do not have to retake it. In the same way, we settle for just getting into heaven and not experiencing God's abundant promises here on earth. Don't sit back and accept a passing "D" when you should be striving for an "A" in the spirit of excellence. Strive for perfection (spiritual maturity) in Christ Jesus and allow God to use you so that your joy may be complete.

> *Now the God of peace, that brought again from the dead our Lord Jesus, that great shepherd of the sheep, through the blood of the everlasting covenant,* ***make you perfect in every good work to do his will, working in you that which is well pleasing in his sight, through Jesus Christ; to whom be glory for ever and ever.*** *Amen.*
> Hebrews 13:20-21

The final step will take the next chapter to fully explain.

Understand that once you enter into this step, life as you know it will never be the same. With this step, you are no longer under the control of your selfish desires because you surrender to a new life in the Holy Spirit.

12. Live by the Holy Spirit and not by the Flesh.

> *This I say then, walk in the Spirit, and ye shall not fulfill the lust of the flesh.*
> Galatians 5:16

Do you believe in Jesus Christ? Do you believe He is coming again? If we, the believers continue to treat Christ's second coming like a myth, then surely the rest of the world will do the same, because we are the salt and light of the world. Christ is coming for a church without a spot or a wrinkle. Let's allow the Holy Spirit to spot treat us and iron out the wrinkles. The Bridegroom is coming and the Bride is not ready. Let's prepare for the return of our Lord and Savior, Jesus the Christ. It is time to spring clean – not just tidy up. Repent … for the Kingdom of God is at hand.

Salvation cannot take place
without **sincere** repentance.

Reconciliation cannot take place
without **sincere** repentance.

Restoration cannot take place
without **sincere** repentance.

God knows the heart of man and
in his heart is where true judgment
takes place.

How is your heart?

Chapter Eight

Dead Man Walking

We must die to the flesh in order to walk and live by the Holy Spirit.

This chapter will focus on step 12 of the restoration process. God led me through this process and I was not sure what was happening to me at the time. I wanted out until the Holy Spirit explained it to me, and then I desired to press through. I did not know what was on the other side but I trusted God and what He was doing in my life. The reason God walked me through this step-by-step process was so I could write this "how-to" manual for others who are experiencing God's refining process and are not sure what is happening to them. Think about this: If Job had not gone through his trials and received victory on the other side, we would not have a guide on how to press through tragedy and understand God as a restorer. Also, if King David's mess had not made front-page news along with his grieving, repentance and praises to God, we would not have a guide on how merciful God is.

God kept whispering to my heart, ***Walk by the spirit and not by the flesh.*** I was not at all sure what He was trying to communicate to me, because I was thinking literally and not spiritually. God had to renew my mind by getting me to read, hear and study His Word daily. When I started doing that, I realized He was preparing me for something, but I was still not sure what. When God gets ready to use your life for His Glory, first the enemy will launch an attack; then God will come in and restore you and minister to your heart. In the midst of God getting your attention, He begins to give you instructions. My instruction was to "walk by the spirit and not by the flesh," which meant I had to die to self in order for God's spirit to fully use me; hence the title of this chapter, "Dead Man Walking." Let's talk about how to die to self and walk in the supernatural.

> *For if you live according to the sinful nature, you will die;* ***but if by the Spirit you put to death the mis-***

> ***deeds of the body, you will live****, because those who are led by the Spirit of God are sons of God. For you did not receive a spirit that makes you a slave again to fear, but you received the Spirit of sonship. And by him we cry, "Abba, Father." The Spirit himself testifies with our spirit that we are God's children. Now if we are children, then we are heirs – heirs of God and co-heirs with Christ,* ***if indeed we share in his sufferings*** *in order that we may also share in his glory.* Romans 8:13-17

Many want to share in Christ's glory, but do not want to share in His suffering. Remember that His suffering included being ostracized, criticized, beaten, deceived (at least Judas thought he was deceiving Christ), lied to, and enduring the death of His flesh on the cross. Some of us have not picked up our cross to follow Jesus because we are still following the status quo of society. We want to take the easy, lukewarm route so we won't have any enemies. If we were true followers of Jesus, He said we would have enemies and be persecuted. But we know He has defeated our foe and the persecution is not permanent; it is only for a season. (John 16:33; Acts 14:22; I Thessalonians 3:4) If everyone loves you and agrees with everything you say, beware – you're probably taking the lukewarm route. Wake up saints. If you are lukewarm, God is going to spit you out.

> *I know your deeds, that you are neither cold nor hot. I wish you were either one or the other! So, because you are lukewarm – neither hot nor cold – I am about to spit you out of my mouth. You say, "I am rich; I have acquired wealth and do not need a thing." But you do not realize that you are wretched, pitiful, poor, blind and naked.* Revelation 3:15-17

To share in the glory of Christ, which is God's anointing, we must also share in Christ's suffering. You are probably thinking,

"Why would God want me to suffer if Christ has already died for me on the cross?" I am glad you asked that question, because only when the misdeeds of the body die (which is suffering for Christ) will the spirit man in you be able to flourish. Remember – this does not take place all at once. It is a process, which will lead you to receive God's Glory (anointing).

People often quote Romans 3:23 out of context. "For we all have sinned and fallen short of the Glory of God." In full context, this Bible verse refers to those who have not accepted Christ as Lord and Savior. But if you are praying your way to salvation in this book, you should no longer be a "Christian in Drag." Once we are truly saved and children of God, He begins to transition us from Glory to Glory. The Holy Spirit begins to clean house of all the sin, bad character traits, generational curses, and anything that is not of the Father. The point I must make here is that **we must allow the Holy Spirit to do that**. Some of us are still trying to run from God as He is trying to refine our lives, but take heed to Jonah's story – you WILL eventually get to Nineveh. Do not try to bypass God, because it will not work. Jonah tried this by running from God's call, which got him and many others trapped on a boat in a storm. What storms are you causing in your life and the lives of people around you because you are running from God's refinement process?

We are to grow in God from Glory to Glory and not in the ways of the carnal man (sinful nature).
We are to change and not remain the same. (2 Corinthians 3:18) God leads us to repentance, to change. If you own something – perhaps a car that you love – you are going to take exceptional care of it, because you want it to last a long time to serve you and look good. We are bought with a price – the blood of Jesus – and we no longer belong to ourselves, but to God. Therefore He takes good care of us by leading up to true repentance.

Do you not know that your body is a temple of the Holy

> *Spirit, who is in you, whom you have received from God? You are not your own; you were bought at a price. Therefore honor God with your body.*
> 1 Corinthians 6:19,20

> *You were bought at a price; do not become slaves of men. Brothers, each man, as responsible to God, should remain in the situation God called him to.*
> 1 Corinthians 7:23,24

Lord I belong to you, deal with me and use my life as you please.

We who have accepted Jesus Christ as our personal Savior have the indwelling of the Holy Spirit who attaches to our spirit man. God is Spirit and we are a spirit in a body with a soul – mind, will and emotions. This explains how we are made in God's image, but externally we all look different. Many times we make the assumption that our spirit man can operate effectively without our intervention. The spirit within us is alive and needs nourishment to operate successfully. Could our physical body survive on one meal a week for a long period of time? No, it would become weak and could not function properly. This is the same effect that occurs in our spirit man when we feed it only once a week on Sunday and not daily. Just as the physical body becomes malnourished and goes into a comatose state, the spirit man can also go into a deep sleep when there is not proper nourishment. When the spirit man is asleep, the physical or the flesh/carnal man takes over our thought patterns, decision-making, attitudes and disposition. Satan knows when our spiritual guard is down and he is stalking us to find the right time to subtly enter into our world. Satan knows our strongholds and our vulnerabilities. He has accomplished this tactical entrance into the lives of many saints and into many churches.

What are the signs when a person is led by the flesh and his spirit man is dozing, awaiting nutrients? Let us revisit some of the character traits of the flesh or sinful nature that are discussed in detail in Chapter 4, "Woe," (page 39). Are you constantly exhibiting these traits?

Adultery
Fornication
Uncleanness / Impurity
Lewdness / Lasciviousness / Debauchery / Indecency / Sensuality
Idolatry
Sorcery / Witchcraft
Hatred / Enmity
Contention / Variance / Discord / Dispute / Strife
Jealousy / Emulation / Envy
Outburst of Wrath / Anger
Selfish Ambitions / Selfishness
Dissension / Sedition / Division
Heresy / Faction / Party Spirit
Murder
Drunkenness
Reveling / Carousing

> *The acts of the sinful nature are obvious: sexual immorality, impurity and debauchery; idolatry and witchcraft; hatred, discord, jealousy, fits of rage, selfish ambition, dissensions, factions and envy; drunkenness, orgies, and the like.* ***I warn you, as I did before, that those who live like this will not inherit the kingdom of God.*** Galatians 5:19-21 (Please keep in mind that Paul is writing to the church in Galatia.)

Now … how do we crucify the sinful nature, or die to self, to share in Christ's suffering and share in His Glory?

1. Allow the Holy Spirit to put to death the misdeeds of the body.

God's kindness leads you toward repentance. Romans 2:4

Only God can lead us through this transition. Do not try to do this without Him, because you will be worse than when you started. It is like taking antibiotics and not finishing the entire prescription ... the infection comes back tenfold.

Acknowledge the misdeeds of your flesh. (Refer to Step1 of the Restoration process.)
Seek God's forgiveness (Refer to Step 3 of the Restoration process.)
c. **Stop doing misdeeds**. (Refer to Step 11 of the Restoration process.) You can only do this by the guidance and power of the Holy Spirit.

You may be saying, "I have been through this process already," and you are right – because the restoration process is a part of the death walk. We must allow the Holy Spirit to put to death the misdeeds of our flesh for God's purpose to be fulfilled in our lives. Walking in God's purpose for your life rains down all the promises God has for you. God's purpose can only be fulfilled in your life if you allow Him in. Yes, God's will is more powerful than our permissive will, but He gives us a choice. For some of us, the press from God's Spirit is so strong, we feel we do not have a choice. I hope you are reading this and understanding exactly what I am saying. Praise God for executing His will in my life – and not my will!

2. Stop nourishing the flesh / sinful nature.
Listen saints, I am not trying to get legalistic on you, but we have to stop feeding our sinful nature with vulgar television programs, offensive music, foul language and the host of other things we allow into the gates of our soul. This is a principle –

"what you see is what you'll be."

> *The eye is the lamp of the body. If your eyes are good, your whole body will be full of light. But if your eyes are bad, your whole body will be full of darkness. If then the light within you is darkness, how great is that darkness!* Matthew 6:22,23

The sinful nature is getting plenty of nutrients, while the spirit man is starving to death and you wonder why you are disgruntled, angry, territorial, and sometimes downright mean. This is a gradual process for most people, and for some it is immediate, but whatever the pace for you, be obedient to the Holy Spirit within you. You will soon find yourself not even wanting to see obscene programming or listen to vulgar music. It will become offensive to you, because you are dying to yourself and taking on the characteristics of Christ. Remember the popular reminder, "WWJD (What Would Jesus Do?)" – it will be etched on your heart and not just on a wristband or memento.

> *For the sinful nature desires what is contrary to the Spirit, and the Spirit what is contrary to the sinful nature. They are in conflict with each other, so that you do not do what you want.* Galatians 5:17

The spirit man is pulling you towards the ways of God … and the carnal man (sin nature, flesh) is pulling you away from God, towards the ways of the world. There is a tug of war taking place for your mind. If the carnal man is being fed daily and the spirit man is being fed once a week, which will be stronger?

3. Nourish the spirit in order to produce the fruit of the Spirit.

> *But the fruit of the Spirit is love, joy, peace, patience, kindness, goodness, faithfulness, gentleness and self-con-*

> *trol. Against such things there is no law.*
> Galatians 5:22-23

The other side of starving the sinful nature is to simultaneously feed the spirit man so you will not be out of balance. The following is nourishment for the spirit man:

- **The Word of God, The Bible.**
- **Attending a Bible-teaching, Holy Spirit-led church.**
- **Communicating** (praying) **with God** (speaking and listening to God).
- **Listening to and watching Christian programming** (television, videotapes, DVDs, Internet, radio, cassette tapes and CDs).
- **Listening to and singing Christian music** (radio, CDs and television).
- **Being obedient to God's guidance.**

4. Now walk by the Spirit and not by the flesh.

> *So I say, live by the Spirit, and you will not gratify the desires of the sinful nature.*
> *If we live in the Spirit, let us also walk in the Spirit.*
> Galatians 5:16&25

Your worldly ways should begin to decrease and Jesus' attitude will increase in you. This process is very personal, because only God knows the heart; therefore many people will not understand what you're going through. Your discernment, spiritual awareness or intuition will increase. You will begin to hear God's voice clearer than your own thoughts. You still have a permissive will, but your will becomes God's will. The internal conflict is no longer a great battle, because your spirit man is clearly hearing and submitting to the guidance of the Holy Spirit. God's Holy Spirit is perfect and He will not lead you astray. He (the Holy Spirit) is like an umbilical cord that connects you to the Father and the Son for your constant flow of spiritual nourishment.

When I first began this process, I did not fully understand the chastisement of God; therefore it took me into a tailspin. God revealed to me that I was in solitary confinement during my purification – pruning, purging, circumcision of the heart or refiner's process. My circle of friends decreased. My spouse could see some type of metamorphosis taking place in my attitude and disposition, but did not fully understand what was transpiring in me. Even with my family and a few close friends around, I still felt alone in this process. It reminded me of when Jesus came into the home of Jairus to raise his daughter back to life. Many jeered, saying the girl was dead and there was no hope, but Jesus kicked all the naysayers out of the restoration room, except Peter, James, John, Jairus and his wife. Then Jesus restored life to the young girl's body. (Matthew 9:23-26; Mark 5:39-43; Luke 8:49-55) God decreases your inner circle of friends and associates when He begins to purify, prune, prepare and raise you from a state of spiritual death.

While I was spiritually dead and didn't realize it, Jesus put me in solitary confinement to restore my spirit man back to life. Many of us are in solitary confinement during our stage of purification, pruning and preparation, but God uses that imprisonment to deal with us one on one, just as he did with Jairus' deceased daughter. He kicked everyone out of the room in order to raise her from physical death. He does the same in order to raise us from spiritual death.

One day I was in my home and God revealed to me a death chamber similar to the ones that are used for death row prisoners. He showed me how I was moving toward the death chamber. I was not afraid because I knew this was a revelation from God. I was in the chamber and realized it was my flesh that God was executing in order to save me from myself. He wanted to use me, but "I" was in the way. As I internally went through the death walk, it seemed so long. The words that rang out in my mind were "dead man walking!" When a death row inmate is preparing to enter the death chamber, he leaves his solitary confinement cell, has one last visit with close friends and family, then is flanked by guards who sternly announce, "Dead Man Walking," "Dead Man Walking!" People will not see you the way you were anymore. You will be forever changed – you will come out refined as pure gold! God instructed me that this was happening to my carnal man (sin nature/flesh). I was a "Dead Man Walking," with God's Angels flanking me in a comforting way and cheering me on as I walked the gauntlet from life to death (carnal man) and from death to life (spirit man).

As a "Dead Man Walking:"
– The spirit of lust dies
– Gossiping dies
– Judging others dies
– Disrespecting others dies
– Rebelling against authority dies
– Selfishness dies
– Boasting dies
– Religious tradition dies (*But if you are led by the Spirit, you are not under law.* Galatians 5:18)
– Manipulation dies
– Lying dies
– The foul mouth dies
– Pride dies

> *And they that are Christ's have crucified the flesh with the affections and lusts.* Galatians 5:24

The sin that my flesh had the hardest time releasing was pride – and that is why an entire chapter in this book is dedicated to this very deadly and misleading sin. I could only write this book because of the death walk – because I was too boastful and arrogant to have written it with the humility that threads through these pages.

> *For we must all appear before the judgment seat of Christ, that each one may receive what is due him for the things done while in the body, whether good or bad.* 2 Corinthians 5:10

God informed me that we all must be judged – because the misdeeds of our flesh and our sin nature are not welcomed in heaven.

> *I warn you, as I did before, that those who live like this will not inherit the kingdom of God.* Galatians 5:21

Therefore we either go through this process now or face God 's judgment later. It is like lying to your parents. They already know the truth, so if you confess, the punishment is not as severe. We will go individually before the throne to confess and repent of our sins. Why not do it now! I decided to choose NOW instead of later.

> *If we confess our sins, he is faithful and just and will forgive us our sins and purify us from all unrighteousness.* 1 John 1:9

Chapter Nine

K.I.S.S.
Keep It Simple Saint

If life stresses and perplexes you, this chapter is especially for you. Simplicity is the key to living a stress-free and peaceful life. God never intended for His children to be stressed or perplexed. He consistently states in His word to fear not and fret not. Why are we so stressed?

> *"Meaningless! Meaningless!"… "Utterly meaningless! Everything is meaningless."*
> *What does man gain from all his labor at which he toils under the sun? What has been will be again. What has been done will be done again; there is nothing new under the sun.* Ecclesiastes 1:2,3,9

We work hard every day to buy nice things, which we must continue to work hard to maintain. When those things become dull and lose their luster, we again buy the latest gadgets. We have garage sales, load up the local Good Will drop-off depots and schedule donation pickups so we can start the process all over again. What stirs us to work so hard to accumulate these things when we know they will all pass away?

> *Do not store up for yourselves* ***treasures on earth, where moth and rust destroy, and where thieves break in and steal.*** *But store up for yourselves treasures in heaven, where moth and rust do not destroy, and where thieves do not break in and steal. For where your treasure is, there your heart will be also.*
> Matthew 6:19-21

If we calculate the time we spend working for stuff and maintaining it, and compare that to the amount of time we spend with God and serving Him, we will be astounded to find where our servitude really lies.

> *No one can serve two masters. Either he will hate the one and love the other, or he will be devoted to the one*

> *and despise the other.* ***You cannot serve both God and money.*** Matthew 6:24

The key to keeping it simple, saints, is "time" and how we use it.

Stressful situations in our lives are usually dictated by time – completing a project on time, getting to your destination on time, meetings, airports, children's practices, children's events or church functions. We rush here and we dash there, but is it all necessary or is some of it meaningless? Let's continue to explore the book of Ecclesiastes to see what is meaningless and what is truly important.

> *I have seen all the things that are done under the sun; all of them are meaningless, a chasing of the wind.* Ecclesiastes1:14

Are you chasing the wind with the goals you have set for yourself? "I want to retire at age 55." "I want to make a six-figure salary in the next two years." "I plan to have a new home next year." "I want to be out of debt by the end of this year." "I want to be a millionaire." But what happens when you reach those lofty goals? You just want more!

I personally have always aspired in my heart to want more and the best of everything. I came to a crossroad when God had allowed me to reach all those goals and then I said , "Now what?" Well that "now what" turned into more lofty goals and more time spent working to obtain those goals. I finally asked God that if this desire to want more was not of Him, to remove it from me, because I was burning myself out. He quickly responded by saying, "*I have put the desire to want more in all of my children, but that desire was to want more of me instead of the things of this world.*"

But seek first his kingdom and his righteousness, and all these things will be given to you as well. Matthew 6:33

It is not wrong to want those things, but your first want should be God and He will grant you the desires of your heart.

Delight yourself in the LORD and he will give you the desires of your heart. Psalm 37:4

I began to want more of God and the things of Him – His love, knowledge, wisdom, guidance, the Holy Spirit, and His spiritual gifts. I found out that this, too, was like chasing the wind, because you can never get enough of God.

For with much wisdom comes much sorrow; the more knowledge, the more grief. Ecclesiastes 1:18

As I began to ask God for His wisdom (James 1:5), He granted it. I remember saying to Him, "I want to see what you see and feel what you feel." This was not to be God, but to understand Him and His will. Oh boy, with that prayer came a flood of the gift of discernment. Some of the things I see and feel grieve my spirit greatly, for now I know how God feels and how He views us. The pain of how we have disappointed Him is sometimes unbearable, but God comforts us with His words – *My grace is sufficient. I will not give you more than you can bear. Fear not, fret not for I am with you.* Be encouraged in knowing that the wisdom, knowledge and discernment of God's will are sometimes sorrowful but ultimately rewarding.

Many of us try to find happiness or pleasure in the follies of the world, but Solomon, the author of Ecclesiastes, says this too is meaningless. The author sounds like he built Las Vegas and all its fun-filled happenings, but when all was said and done, the only thing that remained was God's wisdom. This drove him to hate life because he could not truly enjoy the world's follies and know the true will of God – the two do not mix. Solomon had "been there, done that" and had the T-shirt. He did it all! He realized that when he died, all the stuff he had worked so hard to accumulate would go to someone who did not work to get it. He says this too is meaningless. (Ecclesiastes 2:17-26) We complicate our lives by trying to obtain stuff in order to please ourselves and impress others. Does this mean we should not work, desire nice things or leave an inheritance for our children? No, of course not. This means that your reasons and motives for doing these things should be pure. If what you are doing is for God's plan, is glorifying Him, and is not for your selfish gain, then it is not meaningless.

The Word says that a good man leaves an inheritance for his children. (Proverbs 13:22) Your children will also inherit your wisdom, character traits and morals. We are to work while it is day (life) for when night (death) comes, no man can work. (John 9:4) As a child of God, you should be forever working for Him until He calls you home. That work might be secular, in the ministry, or both, but we should never stop working for the cause of Christ. For God has obviously spared your life for a reason, so don't waste it.

> *To the man who pleases Him, God gives wisdom, knowledge and happiness, but to the sinner he gives the task of gathering and storing up wealth to hand it over to the one who pleases God. This too is meaningless – a chasing of the wind.* Ecclesiastes 2:26
>
> *The wealth of the wicked is being stored up for the righteous. A good man leaves an inheritance for his children's children,* ***but a sinner's wealth is stored up for the righteous.*** Proverbs 13:22

Are you still trying to map out and plan your future, when God's plan for you is already completed? Stop trying to execute your endless, meaningless plan for your life and consult God to discover His plan for your life – then execute it with zeal and joy. If you delight yourself in God, He will grant you the desires of your heart. (Psalm 37:4) God has your job, your invention, your business, your wealth and your destiny already set out in heaven. He is waiting for you to slow down and inquire of Him to receive what He has for you. Keep it simple saint. Trust God's plan for your life.

There is a time for everything. Your life is simplified when you adjust your time schedule to God's. How do we know when the time comes to embrace or re-frame, to search or give up? As we draw closer to God, His Spirit guides us in a waltz through His perfect timing for our lives. He tells us when to speak and when to keep silent, when to plant and when to harvest. God's timing is perfect; therefore, when we are in His timing, our lives are made simpler because God is leading the dance and the stress is off us. Cut out the complexity in your life by getting with God to know His perfect timing for you. Keep it simple saint. Stop wasting time; begin to keep in step with God's timing for your life.

> *And I saw that all labor and all achievement spring from man's envy of his neighbor. This too is meaningless – a chasing after the wind.* Ecclesiastes 4:4

Are we working hard for God or because of adult peer pressure? Do we envy others and want what they have? Let's take a test to see where you fit. Do you buy things because someone else has them? Did you wait in line for a Tickle-Me-Elmo? Were you hooked on collecting Beanie Babies? Do you buy because you want to have the latest and greatest so you can brag about it? Why do you desire to be the boss, in charge, or to be above your peers? Is it because you want to be respected? Do you desire the power to control others? Do you feel good when you have money and bad when you don't? What is driving you to work so hard and achieve so many accolades? Are you unhappy when friends or family surpass you in achievement? If you answered yes to any of these questions, then your motives for working and achieving are probably out of sync with God's will. God has already stated that we are to be the head and not the tail, above and not beneath. (Deuteronomy 28:13) He desires for His children to be ahead of the world in every aspect of our lives, but God wants to be in control of putting us there. He said that He would exalt us, not that we should exalt ourselves. We stress ourselves by trying to keep up with our neighbors, others' expectations of us, and our own selfish ambitions. When you do it God's way, the Joneses will aspire to keep up with you – because by God's design, we are the light and the salt of this world. Keep it simple saint, by operating in God's plan of obtaining wealth and accolades. His plan will take you much further than the Joneses could ever reach.

Because this is a "how-to" guide, here is your assignment for this chapter. Write down every club, social organization, sports activity, community service project, church auxiliary, committee and board in which your family participates – then ask yourself if this is adding to your life or helping others. Is this causing more stress than fulfillment? Do our children really need to be involved in all these activities at the same time? Unfortunately, we are teaching our children at a fairly young age to be stressed out with all the rushing around, and for what? Solomon says that when all is said and done, it is meaningless. Yes, it is okay for your child to participate in activities, but if these activities are putting a strain on your child's schoolwork and your family's peace, then maybe it is not the right time for that particular activity. Many of us are afraid to tell our children no, for fear of disappointing them or dealing with their attitude. We must learn to say no to our children – because if they don't learn it from their parents, how will they react when they move away from home and someone in authority tells them no? We try to please our children by letting them participate in many activities, and at the same time we're crippling them. They are tired, stressed out and their grades suffer. Do you and your child a favor by decreasing the amount of activities they are involved in at one time. In the long run, they will thank you for it. Understand that God has your child's plan for life completed. Seek God – the author and finisher of your child's faith – to learn how to raise your child for his destiny.

As for you and your social clubs, why do you participate in them? Be honest, because only you and God are present as you read this book. Are you involved to please others or to be accepted by others? Sometimes we do community service projects to boast about our charity work. We participate in social clubs to enhance our standing in the community or puff up our resume. We participate in service projects to impress our boss and gain brownie points for that next promotion. If that's the case, we do not get real fulfillment from participating or helping others. God is looking for workers with pure motives. Stop bowing to adult peer pressure. Say enough is enough and participate only in those activities that God is leading you to do. You will then begin to experience true joy and fulfillment. It's time to simplify your lifestyle, but only you can do that.

Fear of offending others is the biggest hurdle for us to get past. Would you rather offend others or offend God by wasting the time He has given you to work for Him? If they are true friends, they will understand when you say no; if they are offended, they are not true friends. God is trying to decrease our inner circle of relationships so He can have our undivided attention. If reading this is piercing your heart, then pray to God to reveal what you are involved in that is not for you or not the right season. He will reveal it to you, but it is up to you to withdraw from it and draw nearer to God. Keep it simple saint. Withdraw from non-fulfilling activities and social organizations. Trust God to open doors for you.

> *What he opens no one can shut, and what he shuts no one can open.* Revelation 3:7

We are in this world, but not of this world.

> *They are not of the world, even as I am not of it. If you belonged to the world, it would love you as its own. As it is, you do not belong to the world, but I have chosen you out of the world. That is why the world hates you.* John 17:16; 15:19

We are not designed to fit in, so stop trying! People are either going to love you or hate you, but remember, it is the Christ in you that they are rejecting.

> *All men will hate you because of me. But not a hair of your head will perish. By standing firm you will gain life.* Luke 21:17-19

Jesus takes the stress of fitting in and being accepted off of us by putting it on Him. He will send the people He desires to be a part of your transformation. Trust me – I know. I went from a bunch of associates in my life to a few true friends. God removed people from my life by transferring their jobs. He also transferred my position a couple of times to narrow my circle of relationships. My life is so much simpler now. Praise God! Ask God to show you if a person is for you or against you. In most cases, you already know who those people are whom you need to let go. Keep it simple saint. Disconnect from the people who are not really for you.

> *There was a man all alone; he had neither son nor brother; there was no end to his toil, yet his eyes were not content with his wealth. "For whom am I toiling," he asked, "and why am I depriving myself of enjoyment?" This too is meaningless – a miserable business!* Ecclesiastes 4:8

Some of us are financially wealthy but spiritually poor. We have much stored up but no one to share it with. We continue to work, to gain more and store more.

> *The ground of a certain rich man produced a good crop. He thought to himself, "What shall I do? I have no place to store my crops." Then he said, "This is what I'll do. I will tear down my barns and build bigger ones, and there I will store all my grain and my goods. And I'll say to myself, 'You have plenty of good things laid up for many years.*
> *Take life easy; eat, drink and be merry.'" But God said to him, "You fool! This very night your life will be demanded from you. Then who will get what you have prepared for yourself?"* ***This is how it will be with anyone who stores up things for himself but is not rich toward God.*** Luke 12:16-20

Why are we depressed, stressed and unhappy? Without the joy of the Lord, it is all meaningless. Start sharing, caring and giving to others in the boundaries of God's guidance. I say this because even in our giving, we should get God's directions. I am a giver by the nature of Christ in me, but I used to give for my personal motives – to impress others or to feel good about myself. Then I got over myself and started to give with pure, unselfish motives, but another vice presented itself. I gave to anyone who asked – especially family and church members. God had to step in and correct me. I was giving to people who were using the money destructively, by supporting their addictive habits – but I did not know it. God led me to the Proverb – *Trust in the Lord with all your heart and lean not to your own understanding and in all your way acknowledge me and I will direct your path.* (Proverbs 3:5,6) He informed that even in my giving I needed to consult Him. Now I ask God whom to give to and how much. When you follow God in your giving, you cannot and will not go wrong. Keep it simple saint. Stop hoarding your finances and start building a relationship with God – because He will direct your path in sharing, caring and giving to others.

> *Whoever loves money never has money enough; whoever loves wealth is never satisfied with his income. This too is meaningless. As goods increase, so do those who consume them. And what benefit are they to the owner except to feast his eyes on them?* Ecclesiastes 5:10,11

God warns us against the love of money. (1 Tim 6:10) It is okay to have money as long as we do not crave it over God. Now I understand what Jesus meant when He said we cannot serve God and money (mammon) at the same time because we will love one and hate the other. (Matthew 6:24) In God's system, it says to give in order to receive. It also states we must sow in order to reap. It says to trust God with everything. When God asks us to give up our finances to further His work, or to bless someone else, He is testing us with His money. Many of us fail this test by denying God's request because we are too afraid to let go of the money. We have now entered into a form of idolatry because we think money is our source. God is trying to get us to trust Him as our source. He knew money would be our hang-up and we would love it more than we love Him. We even gave money a new name – the almighty dollar. If that is not idolatry and serving another deity, what is? God is almighty, not the dollar! Many Christians are drawing nearer to God in order to get stuff from Him. "I'm going to be nice and do right so God can bless me." But God is not Santa Claus. He does not have a naughty or nice list. (Is your name in the Lamb's Book of Life? That is the real question!) We should be getting closer to God because we love Him, not because of stuff. Money is not everything, but God is. Stop making excuses for not giving as God commands you. "I don't trust the church or the pastor with my money." "I already give to needy organizations." "I don't believe the church should prosper." "When I get enough money to tithe, then I will give to the church." *When God can trust you with the little, then He will increase you with much.* (Matthew 25:21,23) Stop chasing after the "almighty dollar," start being obedient to the Almighty God, and the money will chase you.

The more money you make, the more people will come out of the woodwork to consume it. Why do you work so hard for the money? Is it to shower your family with nice things, yet you do not have time to spend with them? What does it profit you if you buy a high-powered telescope for your son and never gaze at the stars with him? Do you think he is going to remember the telescope or the time daddy spent gazing at the stars with him? We buy wiz-bang items for our children – but fail to invest the time to read the instructions on how to use the gadgets. Left alone to play and find their way are our children, the future seeds of the world. Oh, but the religious will say, "They went to church every Sunday and had everything I did not have." Now they are grown and gone, with little or no foundation on how to maintain relationships with others. The material items will be thrown away, and they will outgrow most of their toys – but what you put in them will last forever. If you don't put anything in them as children, don't expect anything out of them when they become adults. On the other hand, whatever you do put in them (good or bad) expect it out of them when they become adults. (Proverbs 22:6) Keep it simple saint. Spend quality time with God and your family, and enjoy life.

> *Moreover, when God gives any man wealth and possessions, and enables him to enjoy them, to accept his lot and be happy in his work – this is a gift of God. He seldom reflects on the days of his life, because God keeps him occupied with gladness of heart.* Ecclesiastes 5:19,20

As Solomon writes on the grievous evil of having prosperity and not being able to enjoy it, he gets to the point of why God gives us prosperity. The author is speaking of prosperity in the sense of wealth, possessions and honor or respect.

> *God gives a man wealth, possessions, and honor, so that he lacks nothing his heart desires, but God does not enable him to enjoy them, and a stranger enjoys them instead. This is meaningless, a grievous evil.* Ecclesiastes 6:2

As I studied this, I asked why does God not enable man to enjoy his wealth, possessions and honor, but instead gives it to strangers to enjoy. Then in the next two verses, it states that it is better to be a stillborn child than to not be able to enjoy your prosperity and not be honored or respected even until death. God desires for us to enjoy life, but not the material things of life. If we get our joy from being financially prosperous, then what happens when the material items are gone? He wants our joy to come from Him; therefore when we get material items and money, we are not attached to them, but to God. Hence, when God says to give them to someone else, it is not a ripping away of our flesh, because joy is not based on the material. Our joy is based in Him who created all things. Keep it simple saint. Receive your joy from God and not from the material things of this world.

> *It is better to heed a wise man's rebuke than to listen to the song of fools.* Ecclesiastes 7:5

Are you happier with your friends who agree with everything you say and always tell you what you want to hear? Or do you really want to hear the truth about yourself? Know the truth and the truth shall set you free. We so often look for someone to pacify us instead of rebuking us when we are doing wrong. As soon as someone tells you something about yourself that you know is true, you take the defensive and get an attitude. That, my friend, is a character trait of a prideful man – the flesh trying to protect itself from being wrong. Rebuke helps to make us "a stronger and more mature saint." Of course, all correction and rebuke should be done in love and by the guidance of the Holy Spirit. Keep it simple saint. Grow up and take rebuke like a man.

> *Exhortation turns a wise man into a fool and a bribe corrupts the heart ... and patience is better than pride. Do not be quickly provoked in your spirit for anger resides in the lap of fools.* Ecclesiastes 7:7,8

In a crowded restaurant, do you bribe the waitress to get a seat or do you patiently wait your turn? Are you impatient with the cashier at the stores or do you encourage the cashier, "It's okay, take your time"? Slow down and wait your turn. There is a difference between receiving the favor of God and bribing your way through life. Allow God to pave your way. Keep it simple saint; be patient, not prideful.

How many times do we allow the actions or words of others to get on our nerves? Allow others to dictate our daily disposition? We need to get thick skin– spiritual maturity – and not wallow in offense or allow others to provoke us to anger. Keep it simple saint. Don't allow others to get on your nerves.

> *Do not be over righteous, neither be over wise – why destroy yourself? Do not be over wicked, and do not be a fool – why die before your time? It is good to grasp*

> *the one and not let go of the other. The man who fears God will avoid all extremes.* Ecclesiastes 7:16-18

We need to have balance in our lives. We should not be overly conceited or cocky nor should we be overly righteous or holier than thou. God has equipped us to know and understand His will, but also to enjoy life in the boundaries of His Word. It is not good for us to become extreme in any one area of our lives. I am an extremist and very task-oriented. Everything I set my mind to do, I do with a targeted end date. When I started to sincerely seek God's face, I became extreme in doing that and cut off the rest of the world. Once God dealt with me and I emerged from death row ("Dead Man Walking"), I saw life from a different perspective and began to enjoy it. God instructed me not to hide my light at home – instead I had to go out into the world. Due to the chastisement I received from God, assimilating back into the world with a renewed way of thinking was not an easy thing and took some time – but I thank God for it because He disciplines only those whom He loves. (Hebrews 12:6) Now that I have my assignment, I am walking through it with God as leader; therefore life is so much better. God has taught me how to have a balanced life. I am extreme only for His will being done in my life. Keep it simple saint. Have balance in your life.

> *Whoever obeys his command will come to no harm, and the wise heart will know the proper time and procedure. For there is a proper time and procedure for every matter, though a man's misery weighs heavily upon him.* Ecclesiastes 8:5,6

Solomon is speaking on issues that weigh heavily on our hearts. Many times when we are hurting or have been hurt, we lash out without thinking. There is a proper time and procedure for everything. We must hold our peace and our angry tongues and seek God's wisdom to resolve our issues. He will tell us when to speak and what to say. We must be obedient to the wise counsel and plan of God, for whoever obeys Him, no harm will come to them. Keep it simple saint. Be wise and allow God to instruct you with the proper time and procedure to handle the heaviness of your heart.

> *When I applied my mind to know wisdom and to observe man's labor on earth – his eyes not seeing sleep day or night – then I saw all that God has done. No one can comprehend what goes on under the sun. Despite all his efforts to search it out, man cannot discover its meaning. Even if a wise man claims he knows, he cannot really comprehend it.* Ecclesiastes 8:16,17

We have worked very hard to comprehend the world and how it is made. For centuries, we have gone to school to study God. But our ways are not His ways.

> *As the heavens are higher than the earth, so are my ways higher than your ways and my thoughts than your thoughts.* Isaiah 55:9

We cannot just study about God. We must get to know God by receiving His Spirit so we can understand His will for our lives. God is looking for saints who are willing to submit to Him so He can pour out His wisdom on them. God's wisdom is the truth of the whole matter; therefore, until we seek Him and His wisdom, we will never understand what He is trying to do in each season of our lives. Keep it simple saint. Do not assume that you know it all; begin to seek God for His wisdom.

> *This is the evil in everything that happens under the sun: The same destiny overtakes all. The hearts of men, moreover, are full of evil and there is madness in their hearts while they live, and afterward they join the dead. Anyone who is among the living has hope...*

> *Enjoy life with your wife, whom you love, all the days of this meaningless life that God has given you under the sun – all your meaningless days. For this is your lot in life and in your toilsome labor under the sun. Whatever your hand finds to do, do it with all your might, for in the grave, where you are going, there is neither working nor planning nor knowledge nor wisdom. Moreover, no man knows when his hour will come.* Ecclesiastes 9:3, 4a, 9, 10, 12a

Saints, stop procrastinating and get to the business of the Father who has sent you. We keep putting things off for tomorrow because the enemy allows us to think that we have much time left. This is his most effective weapon in this season, because many of us have heard from God on what to do and how to do it, but we keep putting it off. We are now aborting our own destinies. God said to stop procrastinating and get the work done, because the complete fulfillment of God's Word is coming sooner than we think. There is now a sense of urgency to complete whatever assignments God has set before you. Do not allow others or the conditions of your life hinder you from completing your assignment. Be victorious in the destiny to which God has called you. Do you really want to meet God and say, "I did not have time to do what you asked of me"? God is the keeper of time; do not insult Him with that excuse. Keep it simple saint. Stop procrastinating and get busy doing what God called you to do.

> *If a man is lazy, the rafters sag; if his hands are idle, the house leaks.* Ecclesiastes 10:18

> *If a ruler's anger rises against you, do not leave your post; calmness can lay great errors to rest. There is an evil I have seen under the sun, the sort of error that arises from a ruler: Fools are put in many high positions, while the rich occupy the low ones. I have seen*

> *slaves on horseback, while princes go on foot like slaves. Woe to you, O land whose king was a servant and whose princes feast in the morning. Blessed are you, O land whose king is of noble birth and whose princes eat at a proper time – for strength and not for drunkenness. Do not revile the king even in your thoughts, or curse the rich in your bedroom, because a bird of the air may carry your words, and a bird on the wing may report what you say.* Ecclesiastes 10:4-7, 16, 17, 20

Saints, this is all about submitting to the authorities in your life. If an authority says something that angers you, don't quit your job, leave your church or leave your marriage. God will tell you when to leave or give up. An authority in your life may promote someone into a position that you feel you deserve. Becoming rich in the spiritual things of God may mean you must take the low road before you are elevated. You might have to walk while others are riding. But when it is your turn, God will reveal you to the world. You cannot get to your destiny by going over the head of an authority, because God is trying to teach you to submit and be humble. You cannot fully submit to God if you have not submitted to the authorities in your life. You cannot receive all that God has for you if you cannot submit to your boss, spouse, parents, pastor or the laws of the land.

If an authority is not where you are spiritually, do not be self-righteous by judging his faults. Instead, intercede for him so he may get where God desires him to be in this season. Trying to change the authority in our lives is a major stress factor. You know why? Because you are trying to do a job that you are not qualified or certified to do. When you attempt a job that you do not have the skills to accomplish, it is frustrating and you are tempted to give up – but when you perform a task that is second nature to you, it flows smoothly. Changing the heart and ways of your authorities is the job of the Holy Spirit. Your part is to pray for them.

God does not want you to gossip about your authorities, but to pray for them. Intercessory prayer is the key to getting the authorities in your life in the perfect will of God. When they line up with God, your relationship is better and your job becomes easier. Do not disrespect your authorities by speaking negatively about them. Your negative words carry negative weight in the spirit realm. We should obey the authorities in our lives – not out of obligation – but out of sheer love for them and for God. Ask God to give you unconditional love for your authorities. Keep it simple saint. Submit to the authorities in your life by respecting, obeying, helping and honoring them.

> *Remember your Creator in the days of your youth, before the days of trouble come and the years approach when you will say, "I find no pleasure in them." Remember him – before the silver cord is severed, or the golden bowl is broken; before the pitcher is shattered at the spring, or the wheel broken at the well, and the dust returns to the ground it came from, and the spirit returns to God who gave it.* Ecclesiastes 12:1,6,7

God is soon forgotten when prosperity shows up on the scene, but Solomon is trying to warn us against this grave error. On our knees in prayer with weeping and jolting – trying to get a plea or message to God – that is where many believers go in times of desperate need. We seldom take the time to praise God for who He is and what He has done. Neither do we invest time in getting to know our Father. Then when a need arises, we feel guilty going to him because we have not spent quality time with Him. We are to remember God in the good as well as the bad times. God inhabits the praises of His people. He instructs us to come before Him with praise and thanksgiving. (Psalm 100:4) Many of us just go straight for the petition list. Dear Santa ... oh, I mean Dear God, this is what I need today. If your children never acknowledged you until they needed something, how would you feel? Think about how the Father in heaven feels when we treat Him in such a manner.

Do you recall when you needed something special from your parents, and you would open the lines of communication so they would respond to your request favorably? I am not suggesting using ulterior motives by communicating with God to get what you want. What I am suggesting is that you praise and thank the Father daily for things He has already done and has promised to do. Remember your Creator before the time is no more. The blessing and favor of God are in your praise. Keep it simple saint. Acknowledge God with praise and thanksgiving while you still have life.

> *Now all has been heard; here is the conclusion of the matter: Fear God and keep his commandments, for this is the whole duty of man. For God will bring every deed into judgment, including every hidden thing, whether it is good or evil.* Ecclesiastes 12:13,14

Why does a 911 crisis have to occur before we reverence God? These verses sum up the whole truth. Obey God by keeping His commandments, for that where true peace lies. Keep it simple saint. Fear God and keep His commandments.

Chapter Ten

Abundant or Bundy?

Are you living the abundant life that Christ promised, or are you living like the Bundys on "Married with Children"? In other words, are you just existing? On the TV sitcom, the husband blamed the wife, the wife blamed the kids and the kids blamed the parents. They sat around scratching, flicking the remote, eating, drinking and complaining about their lives. Are you just living day by day, waiting for Friday to come so you can watch weekend sports, clean house and go to church on Sunday? Or are you enjoying every day the fullness of the abundant life that God promised you? (John 10:10) Many of us are just existing until Jesus comes back. You may have asked yourself, "Why am I not experiencing the abundant life?"

If you have been reading these chapters in sequence, God has already answered many of your questions. Now it is time to put it all together – so we can fully understand why we are still in the wilderness and have not seized the Promised Land that God has ordained for us since the beginning of time. (Hebrews 4:3)

Needs	**Desires**
My God will meet all your needs according to His glorious riches in Christ Jesus. (Philippians 4:17-19) *Based on giving as God has commanded us.*	Delight yourself in the Lord and He will grant you the desires of your heart. (Psalm 37:4)
I was young and now I am old, yet I have never seen the righteous forsaken or their children begging bread. (Psalm 37:25)	If you remain in me and my words remain in you, ask whatever you wish, and it will be given you. (John 15:7)

God meets the needs of His children. But how do we get past merely getting our needs met … and truly receiving the desires of our hearts? We must delight ourselves in God. We must become obsessed with loving God, and obeying His will for our lives.

> *You will seek me and find me when you seek me with all your heart.* (Jeremiah 29:13)

We must fully submit ourselves to Him. We must seek His face – inquire of His will for our lives – and He will give us everything else. (Matthew 6:33) Jesus came that we may have life and have it more abundantly. (John 10:10)

So why are we settling for less than the abundant life?

This chapter is not for those who are satisfied with merely having your needs met. If you are happy and content with receiving your needs alone, then this is not for you. But if you have desires that you want God to provide, then keep reading. I have some desires that I would like God to provide – but not selfish motives or sinful desires, because God knows our hearts and **He knows what we do not need**. When you delight yourself in God, your desires line up with His will for your life. He wants to give you what He has desired for you since the beginning of time. Let's look at some examples of **N**eeds verses **D**esires. Your desires might be different from these, but these are a few of the desires of my heart.

N: God
D: To know God Intimately. To know what he desires and teach others about Him.

N: Jesus
D: To know Jesus in the Power of His resurrection. To have the mind and love of Christ and sincerely share them with others.

N: Shelter
D: Being able to purchase a home for someone else or pay the balance of someone's mortgage. Provide shelter for others. A home of your choice without a mortgage.

N: Food
D: You are able to provide groceries for others. You can support outreach ministries that are feeding the world's hungry. You can afford to eat out and treat others any time you wish.

N: Clothing
D: You can buy new clothes for those in need instead of giving them old clothes you no longer want. You can purchase any type of clothing from any store and not feel guilty for buying it.

N: Finances
D: Having money in accounts to be used by God and for His works at any time. Being debt free. Being a lender instead of a borrower.

N: Transportation
D: Not the bus, but a car of your choice without a car note. Being able to bless someone else with transportation – not just your old car, but something new.

N: A source of income
D: Not just any job, but the job of your choice or owning a business.

How do you delight yourself in God in order to receive the desires of your heart?

1. Praise and worship – Enter into His presence with praise and thanksgiving. (Psalm 100:4) God inhabits the praises of His people. God is a Spirit and we must worship Him in Spirit and in truth. (John 4:23,24) God loves to hear our praises. God's Spirit in me has provoked me to praise Him as soon as my feet hit the floor. Praise and worship can be the action of singing, praying to God, exalting God, and living a godly lifestyle. We worship God when we live a life that is led by His Spirit. This

will produce a lifestyle that is pleasing to God and gives Him honor.

2. Thanksgiving – God delights in true thanksgiving. Are we spoiled, ungrateful Christians who constantly beg for more, but do not acknowledge and thank Him for what He has already done for us? Sometimes my children forget to say thank you when I give them something, then they complain and beg for something else. It eats me up on the inside to experience such an ungrateful attitude from my own seed. Can you imagine how God feels with all these whiny babies complaining and wanting more? We probably sound like a day care center filled with restless babies who have been awakened by a fire drill. Let's stop whining and sincerely thank God for what He has already done for us. (Refer to "The Alphabet of Praise and Thanksgiving" chart on page 94) There is thanksgiving to God in our giving as He has commanded us.

> *You will be made rich in every way so that you can be generous on every occasion, and through us your generosity will result in* ***thanksgiving to God****. This service that you perform is not only supplying the needs of God's people but is also overflowing in many expressions of* ***thanks to God****.* 2 Corinthians 9:11,12

You must understand that your giving is a major key to living the abundant life. **You cannot live the abundant life if you are not giving as God has commanded**.
(2 Corinthians 9:6-8, Malachi 3:10)

You should give tithes and offerings cheerfully as God has blessed you. Many give their tithes to the home that is spiritually feeding them. When giving an offering, pray first and ask God how much to sow into His ministries and His children. He will deposit that dollar figure in your heart; then you should give it cheerfully. Praying for God's guidance when sowing tithes and offerings will prevent you from compulsive giving.

> *Each man should give what he has decided* ***in his heart*** *to give, not reluctantly or under compulsion, for God loves a cheerful giver. And God is able to make all grace abound to you, so that in all things at all times, having all that you need, you will abound in every good work.* 2 Corinthians 9:7,8

Are you abounding in every good work? If not, ask God if you are giving as He has blessed you. You probably already know the answer. It is up to you – Abundant or Bundy? You make the choice.

3. <u>Repentance</u> – Offer sincere repentance to receive forgiveness and change your sinful nature. God delights in true repentance. Let God empty you of yourself so that He may fill you with more of Himself.

4. <u>Seeking God's will for your life</u> – By knowing the will of God through prayer and fasting, you can begin to live a life that glorifies God. (Daniel 9:3-4) Soon after Israel had invaded Palestine in the days of Joshua, the Israelites were tricked into signing a peace treaty with a group of deceitful pagans. The cause for this tragic error is clearly stated in God's Word, "And the men took of their victuals, and **asked not counsel at the mouth of the Lord."** (Joshua 9:14) Joshua and the children of Israel did not seek God's counsel before making a peace treaty with their close neighbors, the Gibeonites. God had instructed the Israelite leaders to seize all of the neighboring land after they had crossed the Jordan. The Gibeonites knew the plan of the Israelites and the strength of their armies, because of the other neighboring land that had been seized; therefore the Gibeonites devised a plan to get Israel to sign a peace treaty with them. The Israelites could not have a treaty with any close neighbors; therefore the Gibeonites dressed in old clothes with worn out wine skins and

moldy bread in their sacks to give the illusion of distant travelers. When Joshua and the leaders saw the Gibeonites and heard their request for a peace treaty, they were wary, but the Gibeonites convinced them that they were from a far distant land. **Without consulting God**, the Israelite leaders made a peace treaty with the Gibeonites. When the Israelites made a covenant or treaty, it was backed up by God; therefore this was for life. These pagans, the Gibeonites, brought only trouble to Israel. (Joshua 10:4-15; 2 Samuel 21:1-14)
Later in the story, the Gibeonites (now the wood cutters and water servants to Israel) were attacked and the Israelite army had to come to help them win the battle – but to do this, they needed more daylight to overtake the attacking forces. Joshua asked God to hold the sun and the moon still.

> *The sun stopped in the middle of the sky and delayed going down about a full day.* (Joshua 10:13)

Yes, God moved heaven and all of the earth to keep this covenant. God knows all and He is the author and the finisher of our faith, and we should seek Him before making decisions concerning our lives. This will keep us out of battles we were not intended to fight.

It should be obvious that one of the **<u>most important factors in knowing God's will for our lives is prayer</u>**. (James 1:5; Psalm 143:8-10; James 4:2; Matthew 7:7-8) In other Bible verses, fasting is linked with prayer. (Matthew 17:20-21; Mark 9:28-29; Luke 2:37) Seeking God's will for your life will lead you to live a life pleasing to God.

(See Appendix A for further Bible references on fasting.)

5. <u>Do what God has called you to do **with a loving spirit**</u> – Do all things in love, because if you do it without love, it is for nothing.

... but have not love, I am only a resounding gong or a clanging cymbal.
... but have not love, I am nothing.
... but have not love, I gain nothing. 1 Corinthians 13:1-3

Your love walk is very important when serving God and His people. You cannot serve your fellow Christian with contempt or malice in your heart; then say you love God.

> *We love because he first loved us. If anyone says, "I love God," yet hates his brother, he is a liar. For anyone who does not love his brother, whom he has seen, cannot love God, whom he has not seen. And he has given us this command: Whoever loves God must also love his brother.* 1 John 4:19-20

Are you serving in a church that you do not even like to attend, but God said stay? Are you taking care of an elderly parent whom you do not get along with because of your past together? Are you caring for a disobedient, rude, ornery child? Are you **roommates** with your spouse, without an active love life or open communication? Are you a pastor of a congregation that gets on your last nerves? Friends, I am going to tell you like God told me – suck it up, because this life is not about us but His will being accomplished through us. God said, *My grace is sufficient* for whatever task that is before us. No matter what the situation may be, if God gave it to you to complete, stay and do it in love.

Let's take a look at God's definition of love:

Love is patient,
Love is kind,
Love does not envy,
Love does not boast,
Love is not proud,
Love is not rude,

Love is not self-seeking,
Love is not easily angered,
Love keeps no record of wrongs,
Love does not delight in evil,
Love rejoices with the truth,
Love always protects,
Love always trusts,
Love always hopes,
Love always perseveres.
Love never fails.
1 Corinthians 13:4-8

How is your love walk according to God? Have you submitted to the Holy Spirit's truth about your love walk and are you working with Him to improve it daily?

> *And now these three remain: faith, hope and love.* ***But the greatest of these is love.*** 1 Corinthians 13:13

We have discussed, "How to delight yourself in God." Now let's discuss what **does not** delight God.

1. <u>Disobedience to God</u> – Yes, all of those sins in your life are stopping the flow of God's abundant blessings in your life. God said He would bless the obedience of His people and He also said He would curse the disobedience of His people.

> ***If you fully obey the LORD*** *your God and carefully follow all his commands I give you today, the LORD your God will set you high above all the nations on earth.* ***All these blessings will come upon you*** *and accompany you if you obey the LORD your God …* Deuteronomy 28:1-14

> *However,* ***if you do not obey the LORD*** *your God and do not carefully follow all his commands and*

> *decrees I am giving you today,* ***all these curses will come upon you*** *and overtake you …*
> Deuteronomy 28:15-68

Poverty is a curse, due to our lack of tithing and giving.

> *"Will a man rob God? Yet you rob me." But you ask, "How do we rob you?" "In tithes and offerings.* ***You are under a curse*** *– the whole nation of you – because you are robbing me."* Malachi 3:8,9

We get caught up in passively receiving our needs from God versus pursuing our desires. God promised to meet our needs. *I have never seen the righteous forsaken or his seed begging bread.* To get our desires, we must delight ourselves in Him and He will grant us the desires of our heart. We should become obsessed with loving God and seeking to do His will. As we seek to please Him, He gives us the desires of our heart.

One day I was frantically praying for God to bless me financially and He told me to be quiet. He said, *If you do what I ask, I will handle the rest.* I will put it to you plain and simple: God is not trying to raise a bunch of spoiled, bratty Christians. God is our Father and we are His children. If He gave us everything we wanted while we are disobedient and sinful, we would never change our bad behavior. He would essentially be condoning our bad behavior, but He loves us too much to let us go astray. You were once a child … or you may have a child. When you were disobedient, your parents did not give you what you wanted, because they would be creating a spoiled disrespectful brat. God loves us too much to raise spoiled Christians.

Let's keep it real – many of us don't even pray to God until we need something. If that is the only way He hears from you, then you will always need something. In some cases, God has given us a little taste of the financially abundant life, and we sold out

God for the money. We served the money and took our focus off Him. The abundant life is not just financial security –but love, joy, peace in your home and on your job. You should walk around with peace everywhere you go.

2. Fear – Fear is a deterrent for God's blessings to overflow in your life. Where there is fear, there is no faith, and without faith we cannot please God. (Hebrews 11:6) Many of us get stuck when answering the call for our lives, because it is so great. The responsibility seems overwhelming, but we must remember that in our weakness, Christ's power is revealed.

> *But he said to me, "My grace is sufficient for you, for my power is made perfect in weakness." Therefore I will boast all the more gladly about my weaknesses, so that Christ's power may rest on me. That is why, for Christ's sake, I delight in weaknesses, in insults, in hardships, in persecutions, in difficulties. For when I am weak, then I am strong.* 2 Corinthians 12:9,10

If we could do it all by ourselves, we would act as if we didn't need God, and attempt to steal His glory. God says that all the glory belongs to Him. (Galatians 6:14) When you give God the glory, He in turn exalts you before men. Do not fear.

> *Is there anything too hard for the Lord?* Genesis 18:14

> *If God is for you what man can be against you?* Romans 8:31

God is the man with the plan and He is on your side. Therefore if God has told you to do something that seems overwhelming, then rejoice because He will equip you to complete the mission. (2 Corinthians 12:9,10) No one can do on-the-job training like the Holy Spirit. He is the great Teacher and Counselor.

*But the Counselor, **the Holy Spirit**, whom the Father will send in my name, **will teach you all things** and will remind you of everything I have said to you. Peace I leave with you; my peace I give you. I do not give to you as the world gives. Do not let your hearts be troubled and **do not be afraid.*** John 14:25,25

Do not be afraid, but if you are, still do it, because the end results will far exceed your beginning fears. You must cross the River Jordan to enter the Promised Land of God, but you will not step in the River Jordan if you are afraid of drowning. Step into the Jordan and watch God clear the path to your destiny. You must trust that God has a plan for the river to do something supernatural for your crossing. Do not be afraid of what God told you to do even if you do not fully understand how it will unfold.

Whatever he says to do, just do it. John 2:5

God only permits fear when it is a respectful fear of Him. (Psalm 34:9; Malachi 3:16; Luke 12:5)
Worry is a subset of fear. If you worry, that means you fear God will not take care of your needs. God did not give us a spirit of worry and fear, but of trust in Him.

*Therefore I tell you, **do not worry** about your life … Who of you by worrying can add a single hour to his life?… And why do you worry about clothes? … O you of little faith? So **do not worry**, saying, "What shall we eat?" or "What shall we drink?" or "What shall we wear?" … Therefore **do not worry** about tomorrow, for tomorrow will worry about itself.* Matthew 6:25-34

God parted the Red Sea and allowed the children of Israel to cross on dry land. Why do you not trust the same Almighty God to pay a light or phone bill? Many people do not tithe because of the "fear of lack." Because of the fear of lack, they are still in lack. The very thing that Job feared came to pass. (Job 1:5) Fear is like a welcoming scent to the enemy – similar to a shark that smells blood in water and is driven toward the smell to devour his prey. Don't fear – because the enemy will latch onto it and bring it to pass. Have faith in God the Father and His path for your life. The "Faith Factor" is key to exposing and eliminating all fear in your life.

3. <u>Avoidance</u> – Do not avoid God's call on your life or His perfect timing by rushing through your destiny. We were already born with our destiny implanted within each one of us. (Jeremiah 1:5; Isaiah 44:2; Psalm 139:13; Romans 8:29-30; Hebrews 12:2) The problem is that we sense it but do not fully understand it; therefore we use it for selfish pleasure or worldly gain. God steps in at the right time to mold and shape our lives and prepare us to walk into our destiny. This comes at a different time for each one of us.

For example: Someone desires to become an entrepreneur, but starts a business before God is ready for him to start a business. And he starts the wrong type of business. God will not allow that business to flourish, because His plan envisions a different idea, at another appointed time. The business owner gets discouraged and begins to seek God for guidance with his life, because so many of his plans are failing. God says, *This is exactly where I needed you to be, right here in my presence, yielded and ready to listen.* Then God instructs the failed businessman what business to start, how to start it and where to start it, and God provides the people and finances to run it. The difference is – now it is in God's timing and not man's.

God's timing is perfect; therefore trust Him by allowing His Spirit to fine tune you for your destiny at the appointed time. When my two children were born, I realized that timing is the key for delivering full-term, healthy babies. If a baby is born prematurely, its survival rate decreases, but when it is born full term (at the appointed time), its survival rate increases. Do not give birth to your destiny before it is time. Some of us are impatient – we push because of the pain (contraction), yet our surroundings are not fully dilated. God will tell you when to push and when to breathe due to a contraction (life's painful experiences which last only for a while). Don't push before it is time. Wait on God's perfect timing to birth your destiny.

Something inside of you desires excellence, greatness, and more. Focus those desires on God – and the pathway to the abundant life will become clearer. God wants us to have everything He promised to give us, but we must first line up with His will. When we do this, anything we ask He will do for us. (John 15:7) Are you living the abundant life, or just existing? The choice is yours.

> *"...I have come that they may have life, and have it to the full."* John 10:10

Chapter Eleven

Who's The Boss?

This chapter is about submission to authority. Wait … don't close the book, because this chapter is going to set you free and align you to receive all that God has for you. I know this submission to authority is a sore subject with many saints, male and female, but it is a biblical principal that we must follow in order to be in a right relationship with God. It is easy to submit to authority when you and that authority are following God's leadership, but what do you do when that authority figure is not following God, or does not even know God? This is a "how-to" book – so instructions are to follow.

When God started me on the process of restoring a right relationship with Him, the first thing He addressed in me was submission to authority. He informed me that if I could not submit to the authority here on earth that I can see, how could I totally submit to Him (God), whom I cannot see. (1 John 4:20) We all have authorities in our lives – bosses, the police, the laws of the land, our spouses, pastors, parents and elected officials.

> ***Everyone must submit himself to the governing authorities****, for there is no authority except that which God has established. The authorities that exist have been established by God. Consequently,* ***he who rebels against the authority is rebelling against what God has instituted, and those who do so will bring judgment on themselves****.* Romans 13:1-2

> *The Lord knows how to rescue godly men from trials and to hold the unrighteous for the day of judgment, while continuing their punishment. This is especially true of those who follow the corrupt desire of the sinful nature and despise* ***authority****.* 2 Peter 2:9-10

Sometimes these authorities are not following God, who is our ultimate authority. When this all began for me, my home church was going through a major transition – a new pastor after

40-plus years with our previous pastor. When a major transition like this occurs in a traditional church, the enemy has a field day. This situation was no different. Our new pastor was trying to get acclimated to the church structure, and at the same time implement a new vision. During this phase, many became discouraged and began to complain and murmur as the Israelites did when Moses lead them out of Egypt. Following the crowd of jeers, I jumped on the bandwagon with my two cents. At the same time, I was going through my own personal sins and issues. Not only was I conversing with others and criticizing my pastor and the problems at the church – I was also criticizing my spouse and my boss. In each case, I was showing disrespect to them and disobeying God. Some of the things I spoke were true, but they were still harmful to the character of these individuals. Just because something is true about a person, we do not have the right to spread it and exacerbate the issue. This is called gossip and slander, and God says these are sins.

Noah had three sons – Ham, Shem and Japheth. After the docking of the Arc, Noah found himself in a bad position. He drank from the wine of his vineyard; then found himself drunk and naked. Ham saw his father's nakedness and instead of covering him, told his brothers of their father's misfortune. His brothers handled their father's shame in a much different way.

> *Shem and Japheth took a garment and laid it across their shoulders; then they walked in backward and* ***covered their father's nakedness.*** Genesis 9:23

It was true that their father was drunk and naked, but they did not spread this information, because it would have slandered their father's character. Ham and his son Canaan (your children are affected by your actions) were cursed because of not covering Noah's shame. On the other hand, Shem and Japheth were blessed for covering their father's nakedness. We are not to gossip about or slander our authority figures, because it affects our future generations and us.

> *A gossip betrays a confidence, but a trustworthy man keeps a secret.* Proverbs 11:13

> *But I tell you that men will have to give account on the day of judgment for every careless word they have spoken. For by your words you will be acquitted, and by your words you will be condemned."*
> Matthew 12:36,37

The tongue is a mighty weapon; with it we either bless or curse. Speaking negatively about someone curses him or her, but saying positive things blesses them. It took me a while to understand this, because I was downright disgruntled with the authority figures in my life. I blamed them for my condition instead of claiming ownership of my faults and failures.
The strong (mature Christians) are to bear the infirmities or weaknesses of others. This Bible verse refers to understanding the weaknesses of others and praying for them, not exposing their shortcomings.

> *He who covers over an offense promotes love, but whoever repeats the matter separates close friends.*
> Proverbs 17:9

> ***Remind the people to be subject to rulers and authorities, to be obedient**, to be ready to do whatever is good, **to slander no one**, to be peaceable and considerate, and to show true humility toward all men.* Titus 3:1,2

God informed me that criticizing my authorities was not going to help the matter, but instead make it worse for them and me, because I was sinning in God's eyes. Also, He told me I could not change them by what I said or by my manipulative actions –

only by His Spirit would they become what He intended for them to be. So I said to God, "What would you have me do when I see these wrong behaviors and motives? Do I just ignore them and stay frustrated?" He said, *No, do not ignore them; examine yourself and leave them to me.* God was telling me I must deal with the plank that was in my eye before I could even comment on the speck of dust in their eyes. (Luke 6:41,42)

> *Whoever slanders his neighbor in secret,*
> *him will I put to silence;*
> *whoever has haughty eyes and a proud heart,*
> *him will I not endure.* Proverbs 101:5

You may have some tyrants among your authorities, but God can change the heart of Pharaoh. Surely He can also change your wife, husband, boss, parents, pastor and even laws that affect the success of His people. Joseph had to endure the leadership of Potiphar, Pharaoh, the incarcerated cook and the baker, but God was on Joseph's side. Through Joseph's obedience, God moved him from the prison to the palace, which made him the second most powerful man in the world. He was second only to the Pharaoh of Egypt. What if Joseph had rebelled against the authority in his life – fighting, complaining and seeking escape from his solitary confinement? Do you think he still would have been so powerful? God's will would have been fulfilled, but Joseph's solitary confinement experience would have been more painful if he had not submitted to the authority in his life.

Queen Esther, in the spirit of submission to authority, followed the proper protocol when convincing her husband the king to save her people, the children of Israel. She did not barge into his office and demand that he save her people. She dialectically approached the King and softly presented her case. He then responded favorably and once again Israel was saved.

A gentle answer turns away wrath, but a harsh word stirs up anger. Proverbs 15:1

What happens when an authority figure does not understand or respect the call of God on your life? What do you do? Let's use the example of Mary and Joseph. Mary was called by God to carry the Messiah, who was conceived in her by God's Spirit. Joseph was taken aback when he found out that his virgin fiancée was pregnant. He was about to execute Mary's punishment according to the laws and religious custom. He loved her and was sensitive to her issue; therefore he decided to punish her quietly. He did not want her punishment to be a public display or jeering session. Mary stated her case to Joseph, but he could not hear through the pain and reality he was facing. We know that God had ordained this birth since the beginning of time and no one was going to stop His will from being fulfilled. God sent the angel Gabriel to Joseph to confirm Mary's story. There is a message here: if an authority does not understand your calling, pray to God to reveal it to him or her.

Often, pride will cause authority not to comprehend your story or even hear your voice. Joseph, by the world's view, was disgraced by Mary's condition. Everyone knew they were engaged and she was supposed to be a virgin. He had to save face by putting her away. The pressure was on, because the fellows were pushing him and his mother was probably saying, " Do you really believe that?" Once Joseph heard from God, he had to make the choice either to do God's will by standing with Mary and rejecting all others or following public opinion by doing what the people thought was right. It is not always convenient or conventional, but we must do God's will. Joseph submitted to God's authority.

Sometimes, you are given information to assist your authority in getting on the right track. Authority is human, though, and therefore will sometimes follow the desires of the flesh and not

God's Spirit. That is why God has strategically put people in place to pray and allow Him to guide that authority back into God's path. In the meantime, how do you submit to your authority without getting frustrated and overwhelmed? Maybe you have a wife who is overspending the budget, a pastor who is planning before praying, a husband who is having an affair, or a manager who does not know Jesus. I am not talking about judging others, but when you discern (using God's Spirit and His Word) they are off the mark, how do you steer them to God's path without losing your mind? God taught me that when I see my authority outside of God's guidance to do the following:

1. Do not speak publicly or privately against the authority in your life.

> *Do not let any unwholesome talk come out of your mouths, but only what is helpful for building others up according to their needs, that it may benefit those who listen.* Ephesians 4:29

If you have done so in the past, seek forgiveness and refrain from doing it again.

> *He who covers over an offense promotes love, but whoever repeats the matter separates close friends.*

2. Examine yourself before judging others. Allow God to fix the broken areas in your life.

> *Let us examine our ways and test them, and let us return to the LORD.* Lamentations 3:40

> *Examine yourselves to see whether you are in the faith; test yourselves. Do you not realize that Christ Jesus is in you – unless, of course, you fail the test?* 2 Corinthians 13:5

We are so ready to clean up someone else's house when theirs may be at least tidied up while ours is a filthy mess.

> *Why do you look at the speck of sawdust in your brother's eye and pay no attention to the plank in your own eye? How can you say to your brother, "Brother, let me take the speck out of your eye," when you yourself fail to see the plank in your own eye? You hypocrite, first take the plank out of your eye, and then you will see clearly to remove the speck from your brother's eye.*
> Luke 6:41,42

3. When you see your authorities out of line with God, pray for them. Don't always look for their failures and faults, but if they present themselves, PRAY. We are too eager to criticize instead of exercising our right to pray. Stand back and watch **God make the changes in them**.

God had to show me that I could not change the authority figures in my life – instead I had to pray for them and He would change them. I was instructed to focus on the good in that person and pray for the things that were out of order; never expose their errors or defects to others, but lift them up to God; then step back, hold my tongue and allow God to make the changes in their lives. This was hard to do, but God's Spirit guided me when to speak and when to keep my mouth closed. As a teacher and preacher, I did not always heed the warnings of the Holy Spirit and my mouth would spew out what was on my mind. This would inevitably bring about some type of fleshy backlash. I learned the hard way to listen to the Holy Spirit and to control my tongue. Pray, and God will take over but you must have self-control and patience in the process. You can even ask God, "What do I need to pray concerning my authority?" and the Holy Spirit will reveal to you what to pray. You might think you have it all together with God, and it is up to your authority figure to work out his problems with God, but if you know his issues and do not pray for them, then God holds you accountable. We must pray for one another. (I John 5:16) You may also exercise the right to peaceably reason with your authority. If you know something is out of order and you do not present God's way, then you are also held accountable. Remember Ananias and his wife Sapphira (Acts 5) ... we have the choice to obey God rather than man when our authority is operating outside of God's will.

4. Encourage them. So many times, we miss opportunities to encourage and honor our leadership, because we are seeking the negative instead of viewing the positive. Encourage your authority and do not tear them down. Give honor where honor is due. Find ways to encourage and honor them.

> *Give everyone what you owe him: ... if respect, then respect; if honor, then honor.* Romans 13:7

Do not harbor bitterness towards your authority figures; instead, genuinely love them. Just as Jesus extends mercy to us, we should be able to do the same for others. Forgiveness and forgetting are essential when submitting to your authority in a spirit of love. If you are unforgiving or have bitterness in your heart, you will submit, but only out of obligation and not out of love. God says do all we do with a spirit of love, as if we were doing it unto Him.

> *Whatever you do, work at it with all your heart, as working for the Lord, not for men, since you know that you will receive an inheritance from the Lord as a reward. It is the Lord Christ you are serving.*
> Colossians 3:23, 24

5. Follow their lead and support them. This one is sometimes a nail or lip biter, because we can give our opinion or advice concerning an issue, but the authority makes the final deci-

sion. What happens when your boss does not go along with your GREAT idea, which you know will save your department time and money, but instead chooses an option that means more work for you and more expense for your department?

a. Do you quit your job?
b. Do you agree to it and complain about it to others?
c. Do you explain your idea, then follow the decision of your boss and pray for him?

I am not trying to make this scenario the norm for everyone, because God might tell you to do "a," depending on His will and timing for your life. But I am trying to make the point that you are not always going to agree with the authority in your life, and sometimes your way is the better way, but you must allow their decision to either prosper or fail. Therefore "c" would be the appropriate answer for this scenario. Of course, do not compromise the Word of God when obeying your authority, because *We must obey God rather than men.* (Acts 5:29) Many times pride rules an authority figure's decision, and one thing I know is that a fall is sometimes the only thing that will break a person who is filled with pride.

> *Pride goes before destruction, a haughty spirit before a fall.* Proverbs 16:18

We must **support our authority**, because unity springs forth victory, but division brings defeat. We are going to examine the battle between the Amalekites and the Israelites for support. First, Joshua stepped into battle because his authority had ordered the attack. If our authority has given us a task to do and it is not against God's will, then we must obey. When the Israelite army battled with the Amalekites, Moses lifted his hands to God in praise and prayer for victory. Something happened when Moses grew tired and his arms withered to his side. Every time his hands went down, the Israelite army began to lose the battle, but when Moses lifted his hands again, they began to win. We must understand that Moses was human and so are our authority figures. Sometimes they get tired or inflicted with the pressures of life. Aaron and Hur recognized the condition of their authority (Moses) and came to his aid with support. They accommodated their authority by first getting him something to sit on. Then each of them held up one of Moses' arms until the Israelites won the battle. What if they had seen the condition of their authority and had not come to assist him? The lost battle would have affected not only their leader but also all of the Israelites. When your authority fails, so do you, but when they succeed, so do you.

> *So Joshua fought the Amalekites as Moses had ordered, and Moses, Aaron and Hur went to the top of the hill. As long as Moses held up his hands, the Israelites were winning, but whenever he lowered his hands, the Amalekites were winning. When Moses' hands grew tired, they took a stone and put it under him and he sat on it. Aaron and Hur held his hands up – one on one side, one on the other – so that his hands remained steady till sunset. So Joshua overcame the Amalekite army with the sword.* Exodus 17:10-13

You are not in competition with your authorities; you are in a covenant relationship with them. Imagine you are handcuffed to an authority and he falls off a cliff. Would you go up or down? Down, of course. Now imagine that person climbing a mountain and you are still handcuffed. Are you helping him climb, or are you dead weight he is carrying? Being dead weight – murmuring, complaining and lending no assistance – drains and quickly tires your authorities. Support them by lifting them up in prayer, and offering hands-on assistance, encouragement and sound advice – words of Godly wisdom.

> ***For rulers hold no terror for those who do right,*** *but for those who do wrong. Do you want to be free from fear of the one in authority? Then do what is right and he will commend you. For he is God's servant to do you good. But if you do wrong, be afraid, for he does not bear the sword for nothing. He is God's servant, an agent of wrath to bring punishment on the wrongdoer.* ***Therefore, it is necessary to submit to the authorities, not only because of possible punishment but also because of conscience.*** Romans 13:3-5

Some of us have parents who are not saved or who are saved, but still stuck in ways you are trying to get delivered from. The Word says to honor your father and your mother. But you struggle with doing that because your parents might consider honor and respect differently than how God is leading you to honor and respect them. God's way is your focal point, and if what they are requesting you to do or say does not line up with His way, you must deny the request. Even in this scenario, you must tell them why and pray that God will lead both of you in agreement with Him. Do you follow them if they are going against God's word? Obviously not. Do not allow any authority in your life to override the ultimate authority, which is God's Word. It is better to follow God than man. (Acts 5:29)

God has ordained authority since the beginning of time and He wants our obedience so that we will not fall into the enemies' trap of pride and selfishness.

> *Submit yourselves for the Lord's sake to every authority instituted among men: whether to the king, as the supreme authority, or to governors, who are sent by him to punish those who do wrong and to commend those who do right.* 1 Peter 2:13,14

This is the analogy that God has given me to help you understand how important it is to obey your authority. Again imagine that you are handcuffed to an authority, whether it is your spouse, parents, boss, pastor or your country's president. Then that authority falls, and the higher he is, the harder he falls. By being handcuffed to him, his weight would pull you down also. Now what if it was the reverse process and he was climbing upward and you decided to sit down – in depression, complaint or outright rebellion? Then you would become dead weight to him, causing him to slow down and become tired. Are you dead weight to the authorities in your life, or are you helping them in the climb? Remember – you are still handcuffed, and you are only going as far as your authority goes.

Now let's look at it from a spiritual perspective. The handcuffs represent the covenant relationship that God has ordained between you and your authority. Whether you like it or not, you are spiritually handcuffed to your authority by God's covenant. Only God has the key to uncuff you. Think about it – we were spiritually handcuffed to Adam, and when he fell, all of mankind fell with him. Now we have accepted Jesus Christ as Lord of our lives, and we are spiritually handcuffed to Jesus. He rose and now we have risen above the world's way of operating. (Galatians 3:13) He ascended to heaven and we also will ascend. (1 Thessalonians 4:16,17) There is a reason for your authority – no matter how it may seem to you on earth, God is working it all out for your good in the spirit realm. (Romans 8:28)

Let's examine the covenant relationships and authority that are established by God.

<u>God</u>

> *I am the LORD your God ... You shall have no other gods before me.* Exodus 20:2,3

> *It is the LORD your God you must follow, and him you*

must revere. ***Keep his commands and obey him****; serve him and hold fast to him.* Deuteronomy 13:4

Of course, God is our first and ultimate authority. Many places in the Bible tell us to obey His commands. You may say that is hard because there are so many commands. But Jesus told his students – remember these two and you have all the rest of God's commands covered.

Love the Lord your God with all your heart and with all your soul and with all your mind and with all your strength. The second is this: Love your neighbor as yourself. There is no commandment greater than these. Mark 12:30,31 (also Romans 13:9,10)

If you love God with all your being, you will want to please Him, and if you love your neighbor (everyone) as you love yourself, you will not misuse, abuse, steal, kill or destroy another's property or life. Simple, huh? The awesome power of the Holy Spirit, combined with your love for doing God's will, IS A POWERFUL THING!

The Word of God

All Scripture is God-breathed and is useful for teaching, rebuking, correcting and training in righteousness, so that the man of God may be thoroughly equipped for every good work. 2 Timothy 3:16,17

Yes, man was used as a tool to write the Bible, but every word was ordained and breathed out of the mouth of God. The Bible is our instruction manual for life. Don't allow people to confuse you by saying the Bible was written by a man and not by God. Everything that God spoke will come to pass, whether we believe it or not. We must use the Bible as the authority in our everyday lives.

Jesus

> *Then Jesus came to them and said, "**All authority in heaven and on earth has been given to me.**"*
> Matthew 28:18

Jesus has the authority over all heaven and earth. We must, whether we like it or not, submit to Jesus' authority as King of Kings and Lord of Lords. It is written that every knee shall bow and every tongue shall confess that Jesus Christ is Lord. (Philippians 2:9-11) You either do it now or do it later, but it will come to pass, because God's Word will not come back empty or void or not completed.

Spouses

> ***Wives**, submit to your **husbands** as to the Lord. For the **husband** is the head of the **wife** as Christ is the head of the church, his body, of which he is the Savior. Now as the church submits to Christ, so also **wives** should submit to their **husbands** in everything. **Husbands**, love your wives, just as Christ loved the church and gave himself up for her ... In this same way, **husbands** ought to love their **wives** as their own bodies. He who loves his **wife** loves himself. After all, no one ever hated his own body, but he feeds and cares for it, just as Christ does the church ...*
> Ephesians 5:22-25,28,29

Public Officials

> *Everyone must submit himself to the **governing authorities**, for there is no authority except that which God has established. The authorities that exist have been established by God. Consequently, he who rebels against the authority is rebelling against what God has*

instituted, and those who do so will bring judgment on themselves. Romans 13:1-2

We should be praying for our President and our government officials, not criticizing them – no matter what party they represent. God's direction for our lives should come before any political party's agenda. We must stand for what is right even if it means crossing party lines.

Laws Which Govern

> ***Do you want to be free from fear of the one in authority? Then do what is right*** *and he will commend you. For he is God's servant to do you good. But if you do wrong, be afraid, for he does not bear the sword for nothing.* ***He is God's servant****, an agent of wrath to bring punishment on the wrongdoer.*
> ***Therefore, it is necessary to submit to the authorities, not only because of possible punishment but also because of conscience.***
> *This is also why you pay taxes, for the authorities are God's servants, who give their full time to governing. Give everyone what you owe him: If you owe taxes, pay taxes; if revenue, then revenue; if respect, then respect; if honor, then honor. Let no debt remain outstanding, except the continuing debt to love one another, for he who loves his fellowman has fulfilled the law.*
> Romans 13:3-8

Laws have been established to govern. If you are following the laws of the land, paying your taxes on time (Mark 12:17), and paying your outstanding bills, then you do not have to worry about the police, IRS or bill collectors tracking you down. You are not threatened by the laws that govern us if you are accurately following them. There are some laws in our country that are against God and His Word. Therefore, we must always apply the Bible, because it is better to follow God than man when laws go against God's commands.

Children & Parents

> *Children, obey your parents in the Lord, for this is right. "Honor your father and mother"—which is the first commandment with a promise— "that it may go well with you and that you may enjoy long life on the earth."* Ephesians 6:1-3

> *Children, obey your parents in everything, for this pleases the Lord.* Colossians 3:20

These Bible verses pertain to young and old children. Not just little ones who are being potty trained. Adult children must always honor their parents. This is the first commandment with a promise, which is, "**that it may go well with you and that you may enjoy a long life**." If you are not honoring your parents, then the opposite of life going well and living longer is what you will receive. This is a commandment, a law which God has established and it cannot be reversed. His Word shall not come back empty or void or not completed. (Isaiah 55:11) Honor your parents, no matter what has transpired in the past. Extend to them mercy and grace, which God has extended to you.

Now let's talk about the relationship from **Parent to Child**.

> *Fathers, do not embitter your children, or they will become discouraged.* Colossians 3:21

> *Fathers, do not exasperate your children; instead, bring them up in the training and instruction of the Lord.* Ephesians 6:4

This is specifically to fathers. God tailored this message just to dads, cautioning them against causing their children to be angry or discouraged. And telling dads to train or nurture their children as God instructs. Notice that nurturing and training the children is the role of the father. Somehow we have swapped roles. In much of our society, there are no fathers in the home; if they are there, they work long hours and do not have the time or energy to nurture their children. This is an ingenious plot of the enemy to remove the nurturer and trainer from the home. A person's relationship with others is often based upon the relationship they had or did not have with their father. This plot of the enemy has plagued our society for generations. Now we are reaping the harvest of MIA (missing in action) fathers. Mothers have taken on double duty, and the enemy is happy to wear the women down. God stated in Genesis that the enemy would be hard after women, because of the fall in the garden. The enemy knows that women are the only avenue for bringing life to earth. We know that Jesus, the very thorn in the devil's flesh, was born of a woman. There is not a person alive who has not come out of a woman's body. The enemy's plot was sealed, "I'll take out the father. Then the mother will be overwhelmed trying to fill a role she was not designed to handle, and the children will be angry because dad is not around or is not the father God intended him to be." Now the children are growing up with a void that can only be filled with God's love. It sometimes takes years before people come to the understanding of God's fulfilling love for them. By this time, the enemy has many on the ropes with built-up anger: *Daddy abused me* or *Daddy did not have time for me* or *Daddy was an alcoholic* or *Daddy died when I was young*, or *Daddy was a workaholic*, or *I don't even know my daddy.* ***Fathers, do not embitter your children*** because they will release an explosion of pain and bitterness on the persons closest to them – spouses, children, coworkers, friends, themselves or even their parents.

> *These commandments that I give you today are to be upon your hearts.* ***Impress them on your children.*** *Talk about them when you sit at home and when you walk along the road, when you lie down and when you get up.* Deuteronomy 6:6,7

This is to parents, aunts, uncles, grandparents and all who love God's children. It is up to all of us who are believers in God's Word to teach the children with whom we come in contact about God's ways of living. Not just memorizing and quoting Bible verses – but application, soaked with love and the understanding of the Word as it pertains to their lives.

Pastors and Spiritual Leaders

> *Obey your leaders and submit to their authority. They keep watch over you as men who must give an account. Obey them so that their work will be a joy, not a burden, for that would be of no advantage to you.* Hebrews 13:17

I must preface this with the fact that God said there would be false prophets and leaders on the earth. (2 Peter 2:1, Mark 13:22) Yes, they are already among us – at our jobs, in our homes, churches and pulpits, and God said you will know them by the fruit they bear. (Matthew 12:33) They are either cultivating "the fruit of the Spirit," or they are wolves in sheep's clothing, sowing seeds for a harvest of "the works of the flesh." (Galatians 5) Is your pulpit shedding good fruit or fleece? Inquire of God if you are in the right job, right relationship (before marrying), or the right church. God wants you to flourish and grow, so He will tell you the truth concerning your leadership. The light is shining brighter; therefore the x-ray of God's Glory is revealing who is of Him and who is not of Him. There is nowhere to hide from God's bright refining light.

Obey your leaders and submit to their authority. If their leadership compromises the Word of God, you must obey God rather than man.

Managers and Bosses (Submission to your masters)

> *Slaves (workers), obey your earthly masters (bosses) with respect and fear, and with sincerity of heart, just as you would obey Christ. Obey them not only to win their favor when their eye is on you, but like slaves (workers) of Christ, doing the will of God from your heart.*
> Ephesians 6:5,6

In this Bible verse, the word "slaves" is equivalent to worker or employee and the word "master" is equivalent to boss or manager. You remember the sayings, "While the cat's away the mice will play," and "brown nosing"? Well, God is saying do not do that in your job. Instead, work as if you are doing it unto Him from your heart. Even when your authority is not present, you must do the right thing.

> *Slaves (workers), obey your earthly masters (bosses) in everything; and do it, not only when their eye is on you and to win their favor, but with sincerity of heart and reverence for the Lord.* Colossians 3:22

Brothers & Sisters In Christ

> *Submit to one another out of reverence for Christ.*
> Ephesians 5:21

We must understand that everyone in the body of Christ has a mission, and we must respect, applaud, and compliment each other's missions, because we are of one body (the body of Christ).

King David's Example

I don't care what these authorities have done to you in the past; you must forgive and go forward. The life of King David exemplifies the essence of this chapter. Before David became king, he was welcomed into the home of the reigning King of Israel, King Saul. You know the story. David became a mighty warrior (by God's anointing) for the Israeli army. He won so many battles that popular opinion and the polls showed he was favored more by the people than King Saul. The enemy is crafty with the spirit of pride ("Don't believe the Hype"), and King Saul became jealous of David's popularity. He was so jealous it drove him to plot the death of David.

The race was on and David was on the run from King Saul for many years. I must pause the story to say – if you know you are in danger with the authority in your life, do not stay in harm's way and risk being abused or killed. David knew to leave the kingdom and seek refuge wherever God led him. Later, David was face to face with his stalker, King Saul (his authority who was trying to kill him), and could have taken his life because King Saul and his army were fast asleep. But David was obedient to the covenant that God had made with the King of Israel and the children of Israel. (I Samuel 24:5-7) Let's sweeten the pot. David was already anointed by God through the prophet Samuel to succeed King Saul as the next King of Israel. Knowing all of this and forced to run with his family from town to town, he still could not bring himself to destroy King Saul. This was the example for us, because David respected the hateful, grievous, envious, and jealous authority that was in his life – because of his love for God.

> *David said to his men, "The LORD forbid that I should do such a thing to my master, the LORD's anointed, or lift my hand against him; for he is the anointed of the LORD."*
>
> *Then David went out of the cave and called out to*

> *Saul, "My lord the king!" When Saul looked behind him, David bowed down and prostrated himself with his face to the ground.* I Samuel 24:6,8

David respected King Saul's authority and allowed God to inflict Saul's punishment. David knew if he would remain obedient to God and His covenant that God would protect David and deliver on His promises.

Maybe you have authorities in your life who have mistreated you in the past. You must forgive them and obey God concerning them. Again, that does not mean you should stay in an abusive or dangerous situation. Maybe it is a parent who abused you and now it is time for you to be a caregiver, but you are having trouble honoring that parent because of the past. Trust God and He will heal the past. The Holy Spirit will nurture you in the ways of love toward that parent. Maybe you are a man who is constantly being put down by your wife and your kids, but God said to stay and pray. Trust God. He will turn that situation around for you. Maybe you are a pastor with a congregation that does not respect your authority and you want to relocate to another church, but God said stay and pray. Trust God. He will handle that battle, but you first must turn it over to Him. If you are frustrated, worried, or spiraling into a state of depression, you are trying to handle it yourself and not allowing God to fix it for you.

If there is one thing that I have learned in this most painful but rejoicing process, it is that God is my source, not my earthly authority. I stopped putting my fulfillment of joy and happiness on my authority, and started giving it to God. He is the source of our rewards. The love of Christ should be our motive for obeying our authority – not the rewards. Rewards are just icing on the cake.

> *Whatever you do, work at it with all your heart, as working for the Lord, not for men, since you know that* ***you will receive an inheritance from the Lord as a reward****. It is the Lord Christ you are serving.*
> Colossians 3:23,24

He has supplied all my needs and the desires of my heart. Authority is human and unintentionally will disappoint you. God is sovereign and He will meet ALL your needs through whom He pleases. (Matthew 6:33) This brings peace and alleviates stress in your relationships by taking the pressure off of your earthly authority to meet all your lofty expectations. Stop waiting for government assistance. Ask God for what you need; then have faith by praising Him for it even when you do not see it. Stop trying to pressure your pastor into making worship service what you think it should be. Call on God to have His church function as He sees fit, then walk in the church with a spirit of praise and worship. God will turn it around in His timing! Stop pressuring your spouse into being what you want him or her to be, i.e. whining to your wife to stop spending so much money, or whining to your husband to make more money. Stop the pressure and pray for what you need; then trust God and He will supply it. Stop blaming your authority and start asking God, "What can I do to help the situation?"

If you are the authority, seek God's guidance on how to lead; then listen and do as He says. God will hold the people in authority accountable for their actions. He expects much more from authorities because to whom much is given much is required.

<u>There is a cost to be the Boss!</u>

> *The words were still on his lips when a voice came from heaven, "This is what is decreed for you, King Nebuchadnezzar:* ***Your royal authority has been***

> ***taken from you.*** Daniel 4:31
>
> ***The LORD has torn the kingdom out of your hands and given it to*** *one of your neighbors –to* ***David. Because you did not obey the LORD …*** *the LORD has done this to you today.*
> I Samuel 28:17,18

As the authority, if you misuse your headship, you could lose your position, your anointing and be replaced by God's candidate. Be careful how you govern those who are under your leadership.

> ***Serve wholeheartedly, as if you were serving the Lord, not men,*** *because you know that the Lord will reward everyone for whatever good he does, whether he is slave or free. And masters (bosses), treat your slaves (workers) in the same way.* ***Do not threaten them,*** *since you know that he who is both their Master and yours is in heaven, and there is no favoritism with him.*
> Ephesians 6:7-9

Submission to authority is not a hard thing when you are doing it for God. The love you have for God drives you to please Him and to submit cheerfully to the authority in your life. Press your way through. It might be tough at first, but God's peace, joy and satisfaction far outweigh the initial pain. Submission to authority is key to unleashing the flow of God's promises in your life.

Chapter Twelve

The Faith Factor

> ***Without faith it is impossible to please God,***
> *because anyone who comes to him must believe that he exists and that he rewards those who earnestly seek him.*
> Hebrews 11:6

As I complete this book, my faith in God is my driving force. He told me to write this book, but as I write, I have no idea how it is going to get published or distributed. I am currently unemployed, but I know the promises that God has made to me are coming to pass. By the time you read this book, I will be in God's Promised Land for my life. You probably ask, "How can someone write a book on 'How to Unleash the Promises of God,' when that someone is unemployed?" In the natural, it may appear that losing my job was a negative, but in the spirit realm God was setting me up for my wealthy place. This is the "Faith Factor." For I have faith in God Almighty and His promises to me. I can rejoice in what He said and not just what I see in the natural. Eyes have not seen nor have ears heard what God is going to do with me and through me. (1 Corinthians 2:9) I am in great anticipation for what He will do with my life.

The first chapter is "The Promises of God" and the last chapter is "The Faith Factor." Whatever God has promised, it will come to pass, but we must have faith in His promises in order to successfully endure and complete the journey. If we do not hold fast to the belief that God will come through on His promises, then we give up in midstream, inviting defeat, and never really know what could have happened if we had completed our journey.

The Faith Factor is crucial in your Christian journey.

> *But my righteous one* ***will live by faith****. And if he shrinks back, I will not be pleased with him.*
> Hebrews 10:38 (Romans 1:17)

You must believe in order to receive.

> *Therefore I tell you, whatever you ask for in prayer,* ***believe that you have received it****, and it will be yours.* Mark 11:24

Let's test your faith. Many of us say we have faith in God, but as soon as the going gets tough and we cannot see a way out, we resort back into our old vices of depression, drinking, smoking, overeating, overspending, crime, or trying to make something happen instead of letting God bring us out victoriously.

- Do you panic when bills are due and you cannot see how they are going to get paid?
- Do you stress if the doctor tells you that you have an incurable disease?
- When you are laid off from a job, do you see it as a blessing or a defeat?
- When God has instructed you to turn right and your family or friend instructs you to turn left, Do you follow God's instruction for your life? Or do you yield to the pressure of others and follow their counseling to keep the peace and keep your relationship with them intact?
- Do you write out your tithe check, even though you know the remaining finances will not meet your monthly household budget?
- When the Alpha and Omega has shown you the beginning and the end, do you get frustrated and quit because you do not understand the steps in between?
- Are you complaining and murmuring in the wilderness, or are you pressing toward the Promised Land with a Christ-like attitude?
- Are you in a community where God has placed you to witness to your neighbors, but you are afraid to let your faith in Christ

show in your everyday activity because you want to be accepted?

- Do you have a job that you do not like but God has placed you there because of a person or persons He wants you to witness to but you have not done so? Are you afraid of being an outcast at work, losing your job or missing out on a promotion due to your Christian beliefs?

DO YOU REALLY HAVE YOUR FULL FAITH AND TRUST IN THE ALMIGHTY GOD WHOM YOU SERVE?

If you trust God, you must trust Him with everything. He will test you to prove your faith and trust in Him. God will allow situations to occur in your life to test your faith factor level. (James 1:3) Many of us do not pass the test … and guess what … we have to take it again. It is like being in grade school; you could not go to the second grade until you passed the material at the first grade level. This is the way God is when He is moving you into spiritual maturity. The Holy Spirit teaches you; then He tests you on what you just learned. Pass the test and you can advance to the next level. If you are faithful over a few things, God will make you ruler over much. (Matthew 25:21)

Prime example: God had to walk me through the lessons in this book, which took about three years. I am still learning and being tested at each phase of this journey with Him. The title of this book has been in my spirit for about two years and the chapter titles and content for about one year. So why did it take me so long to finish this book? It is called procrastination, which is a major key in blocking what God has for His children. I was obedient in starting the book, but God did not just instruct me to start it; He also instructed me to complete it. There is no victory in partial obedience to God. It is all or nothing.

> *Let us not become weary in doing good, for at the proper time we will reap a harvest if we do not give up.* Galatians 6:9

We cannot give up if we want to obtain the harvest that the Father has in store for His children. I must complete this task or I will be tormented by my own thoughts of disobeying the Father in heaven.

> *We write this to make our joy complete.* I John 1:4

The point of the whole matter is: Trust God with everything, even when you do not understand the full outcome. Whatever God tells you to do, just do it!

> ***Do whatever he tells you.*** John 2:3

People did not understand why I wanted to stay at home writing all day when I did not have to work and it was a beautiful day outside. I awakened every morning intending to complete or review a chapter, but the phone would ring, then the doorbell would chime. Someone needed assistance, counseling or just to chat. Sometimes, to fulfill the call of God on your life, you have to turn off the ringers, the television, the radio and sit quietly to hear His voice, then follow His instructions. This is very hard sometimes, because you do not want to offend anyone, but when working for God you are inevitably going to offend someone. The mature and real friends / family members will understand your need for solitude and you do not need the others to complete the destiny which God has called you to.

God has a way of getting you together first, before you can help someone else. I like to use the analogy of the airline flight attendant's announcement. "When cabin pressure drops, the overhead oxygen mask will drop down. If you are traveling with a small child, place the oxygen mask over yourself, then the small child." I always thought that was cruel – what about the small child? The Spirit revealed to me that if the adult (mature one) becomes incapacitated, then who could come to the aid of the small child? We have a bunch of small Christians in the body of Christ who need you to breathe in order to help them inhale and exhale. If you are not breathing, how can you effectively help someone else? This is why the previous chapters are all about God dealing with you. There is always going to be someone in the body of Christ who is more spiritually mature than you are and someone who is less spiritually mature than you. We are here to teach and learn from each other. But how can we teach what we have not learned? Allow God to complete His good work in you so that you can breathe and help others.

In college, I majored in computer science with a minor in mathematics. Equations are second nature to me. Here is a formula to apply to our lives so that we will have dominion over the earth, which God had ordained since the beginning of time. (Genesis 1:26-29)

Word + **Anointing** + **Faith** + **Works** =
Supernatural Living,
Authority Over the Earth,
Living Out the Promises of God.

Word	The Bible, God's Words.	Psalm 119:89; 2 Timothy 3:16,17; Isaiah 55:11; Romans 10:17
Anointing	God's Covering and Indwelling of the Holy Spirit. Given by God for the Task of Ministry.	Acts 1:8; Acts 9:17; Acts 2:4; 2 Corinthians 1:21; 1 John 2:27
Faith	Belief in Jesus, the Christ, Belief in Who God is; Who He Said You Are and What He Said You Can Have.	Romans 10:9; Romans 5:1,2; Mark 11:22-23
Works	Whatever God Says to Do, "Just do it." Applying and Confessing God's Word. Asking God for What You Want.	John 2:3; Mark 11:24; Ezekiel 36:37

When we walk by the Spirit, we have supernatural authority over the earth. Walking by the Spirit is a change of thinking. (Romans 12:2) Think how God wants you to operate and not how the world has led you to operate.

You may say that is a lot, but really all the hard work has been done for you since the beginning of time. Remember that your end was created in the beginning. (Hebrews 12:2; Jeremiah 1:5) All we have to do is get the instructions from the General; then follow the orders. The orders WILL NOT, I repeat WILL NOT line up with the way most of the world is moving. Therefore, get ready for conflict – especially in your own flesh. If your flesh has been crucified ("Dead Man Walking"), then resistance will come from family, close friends, church members and coworkers. If you have prayed them through the process, then your conflict will come from the world. Be prepared for the conflict, but know that you have victory over the enemy's plots through Jesus Christ. (Luke 10:16,19)

The Word

> *Your word, O LORD, is eternal; it stands firm in the heavens.* Psalm 119:89

> *All Scripture is God-breathed and is useful for teaching, rebuking, correcting and training in righteousness, so that the man of God may be thoroughly equipped for every good work.* 2 Timothy 3:16,17

The Bible is the all-inspired Word of God. The Bible is like Ragu, "It's all in there." We must apply the Word of God to every aspect of our lives. For example, if you are sick, search for all the Bible verses concerning healing; then start believing and confessing them for your life. It is all right to substitute your name or the name of a sick loved one. If you are in debt and want to be free from debt bondage, find all the Bible verses pertaining to debt cancellation and prosperity and begin to believe and confess them for your life. The Word is God's promise and it CANNOT come back empty (void). Isaiah 55:11

The Anointing

If you are not packing God's anointing, you will find yourself fighting an uphill battle. Only through the anointing of Christ Jesus can we do anything we set our minds to do. (Philippians 4:13)

> *Now it is God who makes us stand firm in Christ. He anointed us.* (2 Corinthians 1:21)

The anointing is given by God for the task of ministry. It is not for flaunting or showing off, but for ministry that will glorify the Father in heaven. The anointing flows from the top down ("Who's the Boss?"). Whatever the head is doing, the rest of the body will follow.

The anointing is being clothed and filled with the Holy Spirit. Refer to the "Christian in Drag" chapter for how to receive the Holy Spirit. Here are a few refresher Bible verses on being filled and clothed with the Holy Spirit.

> *And you also were included in Christ when you heard the word of truth, the gospel of your salvation.* ***Having believed, you were marked in him with a seal, the promised Holy Spirit***. Ephesians 1:13

> *But* ***you will receive power when the Holy Spirit comes on you****; and you will be my witnesses in Jerusalem, and in all Judea and Samaria, and to the ends of the earth.* Acts 1:8

> *Brother Saul, the Lord – Jesus, who appeared to you on the road as you were coming here –* ***has sent me so that you may see again and be filled with the Holy Spirit.*** Acts 9:17

> *The circumcised believers who had come with Peter were astonished that* ***the gift of the Holy Spirit had been poured out even on the Gentiles***. Acts 10:45

> *He (John the Baptist) is never to take wine or other fermented drink, and* ***he will be filled with the Holy Spirit even from birth***. Luke 1:15

> ***Jesus, full of the Holy Spirit,*** *returned from the Jordan and was led by the Spirit in the desert.* Luke 4:1

> ***When Paul placed his hands on them, the Holy Spirit came on them,*** *and they spoke in tongues and prophesied.* Acts 19:6

You can be clothed and filled with the Holy Spirit – but not gifted to lead or be a musician or preacher or designer or teacher or singer. God decides which spiritual gifts we receive to do specific tasks within the body of Christ. We each have at least one gift for building up the people of God (edifying the body of Christ). (1 Corinthians 12:4,11) Some have used their gifts for selfish gain or to exalt themselves over others. God will not allow your anointed gift to prosper if it is not used to glorify Him. You might get away with it for a while, but God will remove his anointing from your works, ministry or gifts. Example: Saul was anointed the first King of Israel and he used his anointed authority for selfish glory. God removed His anointing from King Saul, and everything Saul did began to fail. (1 Samuel 15:23) He became weary doing evil to keep up the facade of anointed authority. Are you weary in your current position of authority? Are you doing it without God's anointing? In biblical times, when a person was anointed, oil was poured on the crown of his head and dripped to the bottom of his feet. Samuel was sent to anoint (physically) Saul, and then David when Saul turned his heart from God. God anointed (spiritually) the leaders, but Samuel was used to pour the oil and deliver God's assignment to them. (1 Samuel 10:1; 16:13) Oil makes things run smoothly. Is your ministry running smoothly? Are you operating without God's anointing? God will not allow His anointing to remain where there is blatant sin or disobedience to Him.

> ***I am writing these things to you about those who are trying to lead you astray. As for you, the anointing you received from him remains in you, and you do not need anyone to teach you. But as his anointing teaches you about all things and as that anointing is real, not counterfeit – just as it has taught you, remain in him.*** I John 26, 27

Faith

> *Therefore, since* ***we have been justified through faith****, we have peace with God through our Lord Jesus Christ, through whom we have gained access by faith into this grace in which we now stand. And we rejoice in the hope of the glory of God.* Romans 5:1,2

By faith we are brought into the body of Christ, and by faith we operate above the world's standards, because we have a Father who owns everything and He desires the best for His children. We must ask Him and believe to receive what we want.

> *"Have faith in God," Jesus answered. "I tell you the truth, if anyone says to this mountain, `Go, throw yourself into the sea,' and does not doubt in his heart but believes that what he says will happen, it will be done for him."* Mark 11:22, 23

Works

> *Therefore I tell you, whatever you ask for in* ***prayer, believe*** *that you have received it, and it will be yours.* Mark 11:24

Notice with all of the factors in the equation, you must do something (works). As for the Word, you must read it, confess it and apply it to your life. You must believe in Jesus, the

Anointed One in order to receive His anointing. In faith, you must pray, ask and believe that God will deliver on His promises. Faith without works is useless. (James 2:26)

How long will we behave as if we are powerless when we are endowed with the power of the Almighty God? It is like walking into a dark room with electricity, but never turning on the light switch to see. We bump into objects, hurt ourselves and get frustrated because we cannot see our way clear … when the light switch is on the wall waiting to be turned on.

How long will we complain about what we see in the natural instead of praising God for what He sees and who we are in Him? I was driving one day, thinking about the mounting problems in my life, and I asked God, "What is going on?" He said, *Do not focus on what you see in the natural, but praise me for what I see your life turning out to be.* I then said, "God, please show me what you see my life turning out to be." (He began a good work in us and He will complete the job.) He replied, *If I show you everything, then it would not be FAITH.* I began to praise God for what He said I could be and who I was in Him and not settle for my existing circumstances.

Let's talk about John the Baptist. He was already filled with the Spirit of God when he was born. (Luke 1:15) He baptized Jesus and saw the Holy Spirit descend on Jesus. He even heard the voice of God say, *You are my Son, whom I love; with you I am well pleased.* (Luke 3:22) It is safe to say that John had faith that Jesus was the Son of God, whom John was told would come after him. Let's proceed further through the book of Luke. John is captured by Herod and put into prison. While in prison, John sends a party of his men to Jesus and asks, *Are you the one we were told to look for or is there another?* (Luke 7:20) John's faith was shaken because of his circumstance. Let's see how Christ responds to the request, to which John already had the answer.

> *So he replied to the messengers, "Go back and report to John what you have seen and heard: The blind receive sight, the lame walk, those who have leprosy are cured, the deaf hear, the dead are raised, and the good news is preached to the poor. Blessed is the man who does not fall away on account of me. I tell you, among those born of women there is no one greater than John;* ***yet the one who is least in the kingdom of God is greater than he.****"* Luke 7:22,23,28

Do not allow fear or your current circumstance to shake your faith.

> *For God did not give us a spirit of fear, but a spirit of power, of love and of self-discipline.* 2 Timothy 1:7

Stand firm on what God has promised you.

<u>For His Name's Sake</u>

God is in the season of restoring everything the enemy has stolen from us, not for our sakes, but **for his name's sake**. (Ezekiel 36:22)

> *... He guides me in paths of righteousness* ***for his name's sake.*** Psalm 23:3

We as professing Christians are giving our Father a bad name because of our worldly lifestyles. He is tired of Christians getting the short end of the stick, then being mocked because we are operating like the tail instead of the head. We are walking in darkness instead of being the light of the world. We are bland when we should be the salt of the earth. God is taking us through a purification process before He will restore all that the enemy has stolen from us.

> *Son of man, when the people of Israel were living in their own land, they defiled it by their conduct and their actions. Their conduct was like a woman's monthly* ***uncleanness in my sight. I will save you from all your uncleanness****. I will call for the grain and make it plentiful and will not bring famine upon you.*
> Ezekiel 36:17, 29

God said that He has seen our struggle and He has seen the world taunting His people (Ezekiel 36:2), but He is getting ready to restore us to a wealthy place. But first, we must be processed before the wealth of the wicked can be transferred over to the righteous. (Proverbs 13:22) Jesus came to give us recompense for what the enemy stole from us.

> *The LORD has made proclamation to the ends of the earth: "See, your Savior comes! See, his reward is with him, and his recompense accompanies him."* Isaiah 62:11

We have suffered enough by the hands of the enemy and the world's system. Now it is time to forcefully lay hold of what God promised us.

> *From the days of John the Baptist until now, the kingdom of heaven has been forcefully advancing, and forceful men lay hold of it.* Matthew 11:12

At first, I did not totally understand what God was trying to tell me to do concerning this Bible verse. Then He illustrated it to me in a clear analogy. Imagine that a person or corporation has taken advantage of you. If you do not file a lawsuit, you will never receive the damages or losses you suffered. That is the same with the "Kingdom of Heaven," and receiving back what the enemy stole from you. If you do not take the enemy to trial and plead your case, you will never receive a settlement. God said in this courtroom that He is the Judge, Jesus is your attorney, you are the plaintiff and the enemy is the defendant. God says to come to Him and tell Him what needs to be restored in your life. Because you are a believer in Jesus, He pleads your case and God releases a settlement for you from the enemy. Once God has hit the gavel and stated that the judgment is for the plaintiff in the amount of ____, the enemy has to pay up. Guess where He is going to get the settlement? Yes, from the wicked in the earth. It is done, but we must go before God and confess those things that we want restored in our lives. It might be peace of mind, health, memory, finances, joy, a childlike spirit, happiness, a reunion with a loved one. Whatever it is, ask God to restore it and by faith you must believe you have received it. Then begin to praise Him for it even when you do not see it. He will restore you double for your former shame and even one hundred fold.

I have left everything (the ways of the world) to follow Jesus (Mark 10:28), and there is no turning back for me. Trust God by having faith and following through on what He has commissioned you to do. He will equip you to complete the task and receive your rewards. (Exodus 3:11) The greatest reward to me is that I am pleasing my Father who is in heaven. I pray that this book has spoken life into you and I ask God's blessing on everyone who reads it.

> ***"If you can?" said Jesus. "Everything is possible for him who believes."*** Mark 9:23

APPENDIX A

Support Topics and Bible References

Chapter 1 – The Promises of God

God's promise of …

Love - Isaiah 54:10; Jeremiah 31:3-4a; Matthew 10:30-31; John 3:16; 15:9, 13; 1 John 4:9

Forgiveness - 2 Chronicles 7:14; Psalm 103:8-12; Jeremiah 31:34; Luke 15:3-7; Acts 10:43; Ephesians 1:7; 1 John 1:9.

Salvation - Psalm 73:39-40; Isaiah 25:9; Matthew 1:21; Acts 16:31; Ephesians 2:8; Hebrews 7:25

The Holy Spirit - Joel 2:29; Luke 11:13; John 14:16-17; Acts 2:38; Romans 8:11

Power - Matthew 28:18; Jeremiah 32:27; Ephesians 3:20

Everlasting Life - Job 19:25-27; John 6:40; 10:28; 1 Corinthians 15:51-52; I Thessalonians 4:17

Peace - Psalm 29:11; Isaiah 26:3; John 14:27; Romans 5:1-2; Ephesians 2:14; 2 Thessalonians 3:16; Numbers 25:12; Ezekiel 34:25; Isaiah 54:10

Joy - Psalm 16:11; 90:14; John 15:10-11; 16:22; Romans 16:13; 1 Peter 1:8

Freedom - Psalm 119:32; 146:7; John 8:34-36; Romans 6:6, 14, 20-22; 2 Corinthians 3:17; Revelation 1:5

Growth - Psalm 92:12, 14; 2 Corinthians 3:18; Ephesians 4:14-15; Philippians 1:6; 2 Peter 1:3-4

Blessing - Psalm 128:5-6; Ezekiel 34:26; John 1:16; 10:10; Romans 8:28; Ephesians 1:3

His Presence - Joshua 1:5; Psalm 46:1,7; Matthew 18:20; 28:20; John 6:37; Romans 8:38-39

Answered Prayer - Psalm 65:2,5; Matthew 7:7-11; 21:22; 1 Peter 3:12; 1 John 5:14-15; Psalm 34:17; 1 John 3:22

Prosperity - Philippians 4:19; Matthew 6:31-33; Deuteronomy 28:2-8; Malachi 3:10-12; 2 Corinthians 9:6-8; Luke 6:38;

Deuteronomy 28:11-13; Matthew 19:29; Joshua 1:8; Proverbs 13:22; 1 Timothy 6:6,17; Romans 8:32; Psalm 34:9-10; Psalm 132:15; 1 Corinthians 3:21-22; Psalm 34:12,14; Psalm 84:11; Isaiah 3:10; Psalm 23:6; Psalm 23:1,5; Ecclesiastes 8:12; Isaiah 45:3; Galatians 6:9

Healing - James 5:14-15; Exodus 15:26; Psalm 103:3-5; Psalm 91:3,5-6,10; Exodus 23:25; Jeremiah 33:6; Isaiah 53:5; 1 Peter 2:24; 3 John 1:2; Psalm 107:20; Matthew 9:35; Psalm 30:2; Jeremiah 17:14; Luke 6:19; Jeremiah 30:17; Hosea 6:1; Proverbs 4:20-22

Christ's Return - John 14:2-3; Acts 1:11; 1 Thessalonians 4:16-17; Revelations 1:7; Matthew 16:26-28

Chapter 2 – The Terminator

> *The steps of a good man are ordered by the Lord.*
> Psalm 37:23

> *For I know the thoughts that I think toward you, saith the Lord, thoughts of peace, and not of evil, to give you an expected end.* Jeremiah 29:11

> *...How can one enter a strong man's house and plunder his goods, unless he first binds the strong man? And then he will plunder his house.* Matthew 12:29

<u>Titles for Satan</u>

Adversary of God and Man	1 Peter 5:8
Devil, Serpent	Revelation 20:2
King of Devils	Matthew 12:24
King of Power of the Air	Ephesians 2:2
Sinner from the Beginning	1 John 3:8

About Satan

In the Garden of Eden	Genesis 3:1
Asks God for Permission to Test Job	Job 1:6
Tempted Jesus	Matthew 4:1-11
Fall from Heaven	Luke 10:18; Isaiah 14:12-15
Masquerades as Angel of Light	2 Corinthians 11:14
Spiritual Battle	Ephesians 6:10-16; Romans 12:21; 1 Peter 5:7-9; I John 4:4; James 4:7-8
Locked up for 1,000 Years	Revelation 20:2
Cast into the Lake of Fire	Revelation 20:10

Characteristics of Satan

Daring	Job 1:6; Matthew 4:5
Deceitful	2 Corinthians 11:14; Ephesians 6:11
Fierce and Cruel	Luke 8:29; I Peter 5:8
Malignant	Job 1:9
Proud	1 Timothy 3:6
Subtle	Genesis 3:1
Wicked	1 John 2:13

Chapter 3 – Christian in Drag

While we were still sinners, Christ died for us. Romans 5:8
God blots out your sins and your transgressions. Isaiah 43:22-28
Jesus abides in us by His Holy Spirit. I John 3:24
God is Spirit. John 3:24
The word abiding in us. John 5:38-40
Jesus is the way to God. John 14:5-7
Those who are led by God are sons of God. Romans 8:14

Religious Spirit

2 Timothy 3:1-5

James 4:6
Romans 10:2-4
1 Corinthians 15:9
Colossians 12:16
Colossians 2:6-8

Chapter 4 – Woe!

<u>**Gossiping, Careless Words and Giving Bad Advice**</u>

But I tell you that men will have to give account on the day of judgment for every careless word they have spoken. For by your words you will be acquitted, and by your words you will be condemned. Matthew 12:36-37

Then watch your tongue! Keep your lips from telling lies! 14 Turn away from evil and do good.

Work hard at living in peace with others.
Psalm 34:13-14

Thou shalt not go up and down [as] a talebearer among thy people: neither shalt thou stand against the blood of thy neighbor: I [am] the LORD. Leviticus 19:16

A talebearer revealeth secrets: but he that is of a faithful spirit concealeth the matter. Proverbs 11:13

A forward man soweth strife: and a whisperer separateth chief friends. Proverbs 16:28

He that covereth a transgression seeketh love; but he that repeateth a matter separateth [very] friends.
Proverbs 17:9

He that goeth about [as] a talebearer revealeth secrets: therefore meddle not with him that flattereth with his lips. Proverbs 20:19

Where no wood is, [there] the fire goeth out: so where [there is] no talebearer, the strife ceaseth.
Proverbs 26:20

<u>Spirit of Manipulation</u>

*So he said to me, "This is the word of the LORD to Zerubbabel: `**Not by might nor by power, but by my Spirit,' says the LORD Almighty**."* Zechariah 3:6

<u>Theft or Stealing</u>

"I the LORD do not change. So you, O descendants of Jacob, are not destroyed. Ever since the time of your forefathers you have turned away from my decrees and have not kept them. ***Return to me, and I will return to you," says the LORD Almighty. "But you ask, `How are we to return?' Will a man rob God? Yet you rob me. But you ask, `How do we rob you?' In tithes and offerings."*** Malachi 3:6-8

"You have said, 'It is futile to serve God. What did we gain by carrying out his requirements and going about like mourners before the LORD Almighty? But now we call the arrogant blessed. Certainly the evildoers prosper, and even those who challenge God escape.'" Then those who feared the LORD talked with each other, and the LORD listened and heard. A scroll of remembrance was written in his presence concerning those who feared the LORD and honored his name. "They will be mine," says the LORD Almighty, "in the day when I make up my treasured possession I will spare them, just as in compassion a man spares his son who serves him. And you will again see the distinction between the righteous

and the wicked, between those who serve God and those who do not." Malachi 3:14-18

Spirit of pride

Wherefore let him that thinketh he standeth take heed lest he fall. 1 Corinthians 10:12
For if a man think himself to be something, when he is nothing, he deceiveth himself. Galatians 6:3

But God forbid that I should glory*, save in the cross of our Lord Jesus Christ, by whom the world is crucified unto me, and I unto the world.* Galatians 6:14

Moreover the LORD saith, Because the daughters of Zion are haughty, and walk with stretched forth necks and wanton eyes, walking and mincing [as] they go, and making a tinkling with their feet: Therefore the Lord will smite with a scab the crown of the head of the daughters of Zion, and the LORD will discover their secret parts.
Isaiah 3:16-17

Thus saith the LORD, Let not the wise [man] glory in his wisdom, neither let the mighty [man] glory in his might, let not the rich [man] glory in his riches: But let him that glorieth glory in this, that he understandeth and knoweth me, that I [am] the LORD which exercise loving kindness, judgment, and righteousness, in the earth: for in these [things] I delight, saith the LORD.
Jeremiah 9:23-24

Love not the world, neither the things [that are] in the world. If any man love the world, the love of the Father is not in him. For all that [is] in the world, the lust of the flesh, and the lust of the eyes, ***and the pride of life, is not of the Father, but is of the world.*** *And the* *world passeth away, and the lust thereof: but he that doeth the will of God abideth forever.* I John 2:15-17

For whosoever exalteth himself shall be abased; and he that humbleth himself shall be exalted. Luke 14:11

The pride of thine heart hath deceived thee, thou that dwellest in the clefts of the rock, whose habitation [is] high; that saith in his heart, Who shall bring me down to the ground? Though thou exalt [thyself] as the eagle, and though thou set thy nest among the stars, ***thence will I bring thee down, saith the LORD.*** Obadiah 1:3-4

[When] pride comes, then comes shame: but with the lowly [is] wisdom. Proverbs 11:2

Every one [that is] proud in heart [is] an abomination to the LORD: [though] hand [join] in hand, he shall not be unpunished. Proverbs 16:5

Pride [goeth] before destruction, and an haughty spirit before a fall. Better [it is to be] of an humble spirit with the lowly, than to divide the spoil with the proud. ("Pride comes before the fall.") Proverbs 16:18-19

For I say, through the grace given unto me, to every man that is among you, not to think [of himself] more highly than he ought to think; but to think soberly, according as God hath dealt to every man the measure of faith. Romans 12:3

Whoever privily slanders his neighbor, him will I cut off: ***him that hath an high look and a proud heart will not I suffer.*** **(Read in NLT)** Psalm 101:5

Though the LORD [be] high, yet hath he respect unto the lowly: ***but the proud he knoweth afar off.*** Psalm 138:6

Likewise, ye younger, submit yourself unto the elder. Yea, all of you be subject one to another, and be clothed with humility: for God resisteth the proud, and gives grace to the humble. I Peter 5:5

Talk no more so exceeding proudly; let [not] arrogance come out of your mouth: for the LORD [is] a God of knowledge, and by him actions are weighed. I Samuel 2:3

But the LORD said unto Samuel, Look not on his countenance, or on the height of his stature; because I have refused him: for [the LORD seeth] not as man seeth; for man looketh on the outward appearance, but the LORD looketh on the heart. I Samuel 16:7

Thessalonians 1:9 - Obedience to the Gospel of Jesus Christ. Even we as Christians must be obedient to the Gospel of Jesus Christ or face the destruction of the last days.

Revelation 7:9 - A number which no man can count, will be the amount of Gentiles in heaven with Christ and the Father.

2 Thessalonians 2 - The coming of Jesus Christ.

2 Thessalonians 2:15 - Stand fast on the Word of God and do not waiver.

Hosea 5:6 - The Lord turned away from his people because of disobedience.

Revelation 22:3 - There shall be nothing left on the earth that is cursed.

Ezekiel 38:18 - God will show forth his fury to who or what that comes against His saints.

Lamentations 5:15-22 - Turn us back to you O Lord.

Revelation 10:9 - The book is sweet to the mouth but bitter to the stomach.

Lamentations 3:40 - Search out our ways and turn back to the Lord.

Lamentations 4:12 - The adversaries have entered the gates of Jerusalem.

Isaiah 46:12-13 - God's righteousness coming near to the stiff-hearted.

Isaiah 47:1-3 - God exposes our sin, if we remain in disobedience.

Isaiah 47:8-12 - God's warning to the proud.

Isaiah 48:9-11 - God's refinement process of the Saints for His namesake.

Micah 5:10-15 - God's wrath upon the nations that have not obeyed Him.

I John 3:9 - No one who is born of God will continue to sin.

Psalm 118 - Thanksgiving for the Lord's saving goodness.

Chapter 5 – Don't Believe the Hype

Religious factions who sought to establish their own righteousness. Romans 10:2-4

Imitating Christ by being unselfish. Philippians 2:3

Taking power into your own hands instead of giving God the Glory. You will be punished. Ezekiel 28:14-19

No matter how great you are here on earth, those who are in the kingdom of God are far greater. Do not think highly of yourself for it is not about you! Matthew 11:11

Do not bask in the failures of others, because we all need each other to survive on earth. Ecclesiastes 5:8-9

The love of riches, wealth, fame and fortune will drive a person from God into deception. All the money he gains is spent by others and he will go to the grave without being able to take any of it with him. Many times his earnings are used unwisely, selfishly, leaving no inheritance for his children. The man who is consumed with wealth has a hard time resting and enjoying life. Ecclesiastes 5:10-17

Spirit of Pride

Wherefore let him that thinketh he standeth take heed lest he fall. 1 Corinthians 10:12

For if a man think himself to be something, when he is nothing, he deceiveth himself. Galatians 6:3

But God forbid that I should glory, save in the cross of our Lord Jesus Christ, by whom the world is crucified unto me, and I unto the world. Galatians 6:14

Moreover the LORD saith, Because the daughters of Zion are haughty, and walk with stretched forth necks and wanton eyes, walking and mincing [as] they go, and making a tinkling with their feet: Therefore the

Lord will smite with a scab the crown of the head of the daughters of Zion, and the LORD will discover their secret parts. Isaiah 3:16-17

Thus saith the LORD, Let not the wise [man] glory in his wisdom, neither let the mighty [man] glory in his might, let not the rich [man] glory in his riches: But let him that glorieth glory in this, that he understandeth and knoweth me, that I [am] the LORD which exercises lovingkindness, judgment, and righteousness, in the earth: for in these [things] I delight, saith the LORD. Jeremiah 9:23-24

Love not the world, neither the things [that are] in the world. If any man love the world, the love of the Father is not in him. For all that [is] in the world, the lust of the flesh, and the lust of the eyes, and the pride of life, is not of the Father, but is of the world. And the world passeth away, and the lust thereof: but he that doeth the will of God abideth forever. I John 2:15-17

For whosoever exalteth himself shall be abased; and he that humbleth himself shall be exalted. Luke 14:11

The pride of thine heart hath deceived thee, thou that dwellest in the clefts of the rock, whose habitation [is] high; that saith in his heart, Who shall bring me down to the ground? Though thou exalt [thyself] as the eagle, and though thou set thy nest among the stars, thence will I bring thee down, saith the LORD. Obadiah 1:3-4

[When] pride cometh, then cometh shame: but with the lowly [is] wisdom. Proverbs 11:2

Every one [that is] proud in heart [is] an abomination to the LORD: [though] hand [join] in hand, he shall not be unpunished. Proverbs 16:5

Pride [goeth] before destruction, and an haughty spirit before a fall. Better [it is to be] of an humble spirit with the lowly, than to divide the spoil with the proud. ("Pride comes before the fall.") Proverbs 16:18-19

For I say, through the grace given unto me, to every man that is among you, not to think [of himself] more highly than he ought to think; but to think soberly, according as God hath dealt to every man the measure of faith. Romans 12:3

Whose privity slandereth his neighbor, him will I cut off: him that hath an high look and a proud heart will not I suffer. Psalm101:5

Though the LORD [be] high, yet hath he respect unto the lowly: but the proud he knoweth afar off. Psalm 138:6

Likewise, ye younger, submit yourself unto the elder. Yea, all of you be subject one to another, and be clothed with humility: for God resisteth the proud, and giveth grace to the humble. I Peter 5:5

Talk no more so exceeding proudly; let [not] arrogancy come out of your mouth: for the LORD [is] a God of knowledge, and by him actions are weighed. I Samuel 2:3

But the LORD said unto Samuel, Look not on his countenance, or on the height of his stature; because I have refused him: for [the LORD seeth] not as man seeth; for man looketh on the outward appearance, but the LORD looketh on the heart. I Samuel 16:7

Chapter 10 – Abundant or Bundy?

– **Meaning of Fasting:** Tvath (Aramaic) from a root corresponding to tavath; hunger (as twisting) – fasting. To fast is to abstain for a period of time from some important and necessary activity in our lives. **Matthew 4:2-4**

– **Purpose for Fasting:** This is done so we can spend that time in prayer before God.
Confession and Repentance: **Nehemiah 9:1-2**
Atonement and Restoration: **Joel 2:12**
Praying for the Sick: **Psalm 35:13**
Deliverance: **Psalm 109:19-24**
Confirmation and Guidance: **Esther 9:31**
The Cares of the Church: **2 Corinthians 11:27-28**
Appointment of Leaders: **Acts 14:23**

– **Kinds of Fasting:** One may, for a time, refrain from the following:
Sleep: **2 Corinthians 6:5; 11:27**
Marital Sex: **1Corinthians 7:1-5**
Food: **Matthew 4:1-2**

– **Other Things that Accompany Fasting:**
Prayer: **Luke 2:37**
Humility: **Nehemiah 9:1**
Confession: **Nehemiah 9:1-2**
Mourning: **Joel 2:12**

– **Examples of Biblical Fasting:**
Moses: **Deuteronomy 9:9, 18, 25-29**
Elijah: **1 Kings 19:8**
Daniel: **Daniel 9:3; 10:3**
Ezra: **Ezra 10:6**
Nehemiah: **Nehemiah 1:4**

Esther: **Esther 9:31**

Paul: **2 Corinthians 6:5; 11:27**

Anna: **Luke 2:36-37**

Jesus: **Matthew 4:1-11**

– **Results of Fasting: ANSWERED PRAYER- Acts 10:30-35**

APPENDIX B

Sources Cited

Compton's Interactive Bible NIV. Copyright © 1994, 1995, 1996 SoftKey Multimedia Inc. All Rights Reserved

The Holy Bible, New International Version. Copyright © 1973, 1978, 1984 by International Bible Society

Holman Bible Dictionary, Copyright © 1991 Holman Bible Publishers

The Complete Multimedia Bible Based on the King James Version. Copyright © 1995-1998 Learning Company Properties Inc.

The Holy Bible, New King James Version Copyright © 1982 by Thomas Nelson, Inc.

The Names of God Copyright © 1997